DATE DUE

JAN 2 7 2016			

Demco, Inc. 38-293

✶ ✶ ✶ ✶ ✶ ✶ ✶ ✶ ✶ ✶ ✶ ✶ ✶ ✶ ✶ ✶

BASEBALL SUPERSTARS

Johnny Damon

✶ ✶ ✶ ✶ ✶ ✶ ✶ ✶ ✶ ✶ ✶ ✶ ✶ ✶ ✶ ✶

Hank Aaron
Ty Cobb
Johnny Damon
Lou Gehrig
Rickey Henderson
Derek Jeter
Randy Johnson
Andruw Jones
Mickey Mantle
Roger Maris

Mike Piazza
Kirby Puckett
Albert Pujols
Mariano Rivera
Jackie Robinson
Babe Ruth
Curt Schilling
Ichiro Suzuki
Bernie Williams
Ted Williams

BASEBALL SUPERSTARS

Johnny Damon

Brian O'Connell

CHELSEA HOUSE
PUBLISHERS
An imprint of Infobase Publishing

JOHNNY DAMON
Copyright © 2008 by Infobase Publishing

All rights reserved. No part of this book may be reproduced or utilized in any form or by any means, electronic or mechanical, including photocopying, recording, or by any information storage or retrieval systems, without permission in writing from the publisher. For information, contact:

Chelsea House
An imprint of Infobase Publishing
132 West 31st Street
New York NY 10001

Library of Congress Cataloging-in-Publication Data
O'Connell, Brian, 1959-
  Johnny Damon / Brian O'Connell.
    p. cm.— (Baseball superstars)
  Includes bibliographical references and index.
  ISBN 978-0-7910-9646-8 (hardcover)
  1. Damon, Johnny. 2. Baseball players—Biography. 3. Boston Red Sox (Baseball team)
I. Title.
  GV865.D36O36 2008
  796.357092—dc22
  [B]   2007036303

Chelsea House books are available at special discounts when purchased in bulk quantities for businesses, associations, institutions, or sales promotions. Please call our Special Sales Department in New York at (212) 967-8800 or (800) 322-8755.

You can find Chelsea House on the World Wide Web at http://www.chelseahouse.com

Series design by Erik Lindstrom
Cover design by Ben Peterson

Printed in the United States of America

Bang EJB 10 9 8 7 6 5 4 3 2 1

This book is printed on acid-free paper.

All links and Web addresses were checked and verified to be correct at the time of publication. Because of the dynamic nature of the Web, some addresses and links may have changed since publication and may no longer be valid.

CONTENTS

c

Yankee Killer

Johnny Damon ambled up to home plate, blocking out the steady boos and shrill catcalls from seemingly every one of the 56,000-plus fans packing Yankee Stadium.

The date was October 20, 2004, and only one year before, Damon had experienced one of the most crushing disappointments of his life: The Yankees had stormed back from a Game 7 deficit against Damon's Boston Red Sox and pitcher Pedro Martínez, winning the American League Championship Series with a walk-off home run in the eleventh inning.

Damon remembered the sickening feeling in the pit of his stomach while watching the Yankee players whooping and hollering on the hallowed green diamond of Yankee Stadium. The knowledge that generation after generation of talented

Red Sox teams had suffered the same fate, right here on the same turf, did not ease the pain.

A COMEBACK TO REMEMBER

But tonight—tonight would be different. After all, the Red Sox had fashioned a historic comeback of their own in the last week. Seemingly given up for dead, the BoSox, led by colorful characters like Damon, Martínez, pitching ace Curt Schilling, and sluggers Manny Ramírez and David Ortiz, had overcome a three-games-to-zero deficit against the Yankees in the American League Championship Series.

There was Ortiz's clutch home run to win Game 4 in the twelfth inning, followed by his bloop single for the ages in Game 5. That hit had sent 35,000 members of Red Sox Nation home from Fenway Park, throats raw from the yelling and screaming, but happy that there would be a Game 6 in New York.

And what a game it was. The heroic Schilling, pitching with a bandaged, blood-soaked suture that stained the sock covering his right ankle, gamely held the Yankees to two measly runs as the Red Sox tied up the series in what baseball writers universally declared an "instant classic."

Damon thought about that. He had played below average in the series, batting only .103 coming into this last game, but he knew he was in a position to make amends. To make history. After all, no team in the history of Major League Baseball had ever climbed all the way back from such a hole.

Clearly, Damon thought, the tide was turning in the Red Sox's favor.

Already in Game 7, the Sox had a 2-0 lead on the hated Bronx Bombers. Damon himself had singled to lead off the game, but he had been thrown out at home after a double by Ramírez. But, like the Red Sox fortunes all year, Ortiz had Damon's back, hitting a home run on the very next pitch to stake the BoSox to a two-run lead.

The big, blond Red Sox pitcher, Derek Lowe, had pitched a quiet first inning, and Damon thought that the lanky right-hander had his "good stuff" that night. "If we can only get him some runs," Damon thought.

That would not be easy. The Yankees' staff ace, Kevin Brown, had started the game, and Damon knew that Brown's heavy sinker and nasty cut fastball could present big problems for the Red Sox hitters, even after Ortiz's first-inning bomb.

But Red Sox first baseman Kevin Millar had opened the second inning with a single, and third baseman Bill Mueller had worked Brown for a free pass. Brown faltered again with the next batter, shortstop Orlando Cabrera, walking him as well.

Suddenly the bases were loaded, and the Yankee fans sensed a big moment. That Damon, reviled in New York for his long, wavy, jet-black hair and his Grizzly Adams beard, was up only heightened the drama. "If we can only get him some runs," Damon thought again.

Well, here was an excellent opportunity to do just that. A base hit would probably score two runs and give the Red Sox a 4-0 lead. Not insurmountable, but certainly an uphill fight for even the talented Yankees.

A CRUCIAL AT-BAT

It would be the biggest at-bat of Johnny Damon's life. The son of an army staff sergeant, Damon felt as if his entire life had risen up to meet this game and this at-bat. Moved from location to location as an army brat kid, Damon had lived everywhere from the rocky island of Okinawa in the Pacific to the lush hills of Fort Campbell, Kentucky.

His mother, born and raised in Thailand, captivated by the all-American image of Disney World, persuaded her husband to retire and start a new life with Johnny and his older brother, James, in Orlando, Florida.

Playing baseball with his friends "all day long, day after day" as Damon recalled, honed his competitive skills. By age 13, Johnny had the ripped physique of a 25-year-old, and he caught the interest of local baseball scouts—or "birddogs," as baseball insiders call them.

What they saw was a young teenager who could run like a deer and hit the cover off the ball. By the time Johnny arrived at Dr. Phillips High School in Orlando, his fate was set. He would be a baseball player—a highly sought-after one who would make the leap from the minor leagues to the major leagues without a beat, winding up as one of the most successful and popular players of his day.

But that wasn't on Damon's mind as he strode up to the plate that night in Yankee Stadium. He tapped his cleated instep with his black, 34-inch Rawlings "Big Stick" baseball bat and stared intently at the new Yankees pitcher, Javier Vázquez, who had replaced the struggling Brown.

Damon had only faced Vázquez a few times, but it was enough to create a decent "book" on the Yankee hurler. Damon knew that Vázquez liked to keep hitters guessing by changing speeds and throwing their timing out of whack. But a good changeup pitcher needs to set up the pitch with a fastball, to keep batters honest.

Damon guessed fastball—on the inside of the plate so he couldn't use his bat speed and powerful forearms to reach across the plate and hammer the ball into the outfield gap or, worse for Vázquez and the Yankees, over the wall.

"C'mon, big fella, pitch it in. Let me see it," Damon recalled thinking. Sure enough, Vázquez grooved a fastball in, tailing toward Damon's wrists. In most cases, "jamming" a hitter inside on the wrists results in a harmless ground ball or a pop-up in the infield. But Damon, thanks to hours of work in the batting cage, was able to adjust his balance and swing hard.

The moment he heard the crack of the bat against the ball, Damon knew it had a chance to go out. Yankee Stadium's

Johnny Damon connects on a grand slam in Game 7 of the 2004 American League Championship Series. His second-inning home run gave the Boston Red Sox a 6-0 lead against the New York Yankees. Two innings later, Damon hit another round-tripper.

famously short right-field porch improved those odds, and Damon watched in seemingly slow motion as the ball disappeared over the wall into the bleachers, an awkward souvenir for a deflated Yankee fan. A grand slam. A four-bagger. A grand salami. The biggest hit a batter could ever ask for, and Johnny Damon had done it in front of a hostile crowd and a worldwide television audience of tens of millions of people.

Circling the bases, Damon secretly eyed the scoreboard, taking pains to make sure he did not smile. It was a grand slam, all right, and the Red Sox were now up 6-0 over their hated rivals. The game, though, was not over yet—not with a studded Yankee lineup featuring future Hall of Famers like Derek Jeter and Alex Rodriguez. Nothing to smile about yet.

☆ ☆ ☆ ☆ ☆

IN HIS OWN WORDS

The grand slam that Johnny Damon struck in the second inning of Game 7 of the American League Championship Series helped propel the Red Sox to victory. In his book, *Idiot: Beating "The Curse" and Enjoying the Game of Life*, Damon wrote about his spectacular hit:

> That home run is always going to be part of the history of Boston, the history of baseball. I started the season with long hair and a beard, and then after I hit that home run, for some fans I became God—or maybe I should say Jesus. It's hyperbole, obviously, but I'm telling you the feeling. It was just incredible. Thousands of Red Sox fans had been led to believe the Sox would never win the big game during their lifetimes. Well, here was proof that their lives were about to change.

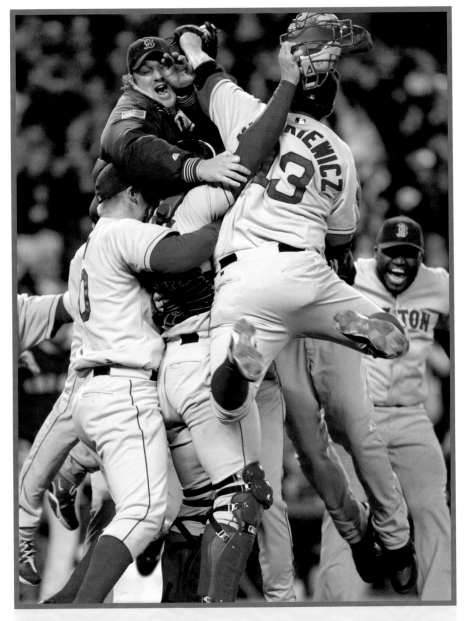

Players from the Red Sox celebrated after the last out in the final game of the 2004 American League Championship Series. In Game 7, the Red Sox not only beat New York, 10-3, they also beat many demons of the past. The Red Sox became the first major-league team ever to win a seven-game postseason series after trailing three games to none.

IT'S OUTTA HERE, AGAIN

Momentum, though, was on Boston's side. Two innings later, Damon did it again, walloping a Vázquez fastball even deeper into the right-field stands. It was now 8-1 Red Sox.

Lowe, the big right-hander, took over from there and shut the Bronx Bombers down in style. A weak ground-out by Rubén Sierra sealed the Yankees' fate and with it a hurdle in overcoming the famous Red Sox "Curse of the Bambino"—in which legend has it that the Red Sox could never win the World Series after trading superstar Babe Ruth to the Yankees nearly 85 years before.

There would be no curse that magical night in New York City, if ever again. Johnny Damon found himself on top of a pile of joyous Red Sox players, right on top of the pitcher's mound at Yankee Stadium—the same mound where Yankee hurlers had stymied the Red Sox in big game after big game.

Yes, tonight the Red Sox were the ones dancing on the other guys' turf. They were the ones celebrating in front of the other guys' stunned fans. They were champions.

All thanks to one of the most popular players in Red Sox history—Johnny Damon, the army brat from Orlando.

From Army Brat to Baseball Prodigy

Johnny Damon was born on November 5, 1973, at an army base in Fort Riley, Kansas. His father, Jimmy, was serving in the United States Army and had recently moved from Thailand, where he had met Damon's mother, Yome, a nurse of Thai descent who was helping army troops during the Vietnam War. Jimmy and Yome were married in Thailand, and Yome gave birth there to Damon's older brother, James, in 1971 before the family moved back to the United States.

Though some would call him an "Army brat," Johnny was anything but entitled growing up. Like many children of military parents, he would often move from place to place, sometimes staying in one spot for no longer than a few years.

Shortly after he was born, Johnny and his family moved from Kansas to Germany for a brief time and then to Okinawa,

Japan, where they lived for several years. During those years, he occasionally accompanied his mother on trips to see her parents in Thailand.

Johnny enjoyed living in Okinawa. He and his mother went for walks along the island's rocky beaches and caught lobsters to take home. Even at an early age, Johnny was fearless. He sometimes would get pinched trying to play with the lobsters. Instead of leaving the crustaceans alone, however, he tried to play with them even more to see just how tough they were. Johnny was always probing, always curious about any potential weak spots in a competitor—even if he was trying to pick off a lobster or two. These traits would serve him well later in batter's boxes across the American League, where he would try to probe the few weaknesses of pitching greats like Randy Johnson, Barry Zito, and Pedro Martínez (before Damon became his teammate on the Red Sox).

Though he never got in big trouble, Johnny was usually allowed to follow his curiosity as a child. His parents let him do things, even if they might be dangerous, so he could learn to watch out for himself. Years later, at age 12, Johnny was allowed to drive his father's car.

BACK TO THE STATES

When Johnny was 4, his family moved once again—this time to Fort Campbell, Kentucky, where his father was stationed. It was there that Johnny first started to show signs of his athleticism. Left alone at home with his mother while his brother went to school and his father worked, he fought his boredom by running laps around the family's house.

Johnny was also close to getting his first taste of baseball at Fort Campbell. His mother had signed James and Johnny up for a local baseball league—Johnny was going to play T-ball, and James was going to play baseball. The family, though, moved once again before the season could start.

Luckily for Johnny, the family's next relocation would be the last one for a long time. His father was ready to leave the Army after serving for 20 years and 20 days, and his mother, a Disney fan, wanted to move to either California or Florida, where the entertainment giant's two famous theme parks are located.

Johnny's parents eventually settled on Orlando, Florida. Several of Yome's friends from Thailand lived in the area. The city also provided employment for Johnny's parents; his father became a security guard at a local mall, and his mother held multiple jobs as a bookbinder and a housekeeper. Although Johnny largely had free rein with both of his parents working, he still had to answer to his older brother, James, who kept a bit of a short leash on Johnny.

Johnny took to his new surroundings, meeting several new friends (including a young Joey Fatone, who would go on to stardom as a member of the musical group *NSYNC) and exploring the lakes of central Florida. Living near Lake Buena Vista, Johnny and his friends usually played in the empty construction sites and fields in the shadows of the Disney World empire. As a result, getting dirty became an early pastime for Johnny.

Johnny liked to make new friends but, deep down, he was a quiet kid. For years, Johnny battled a stuttering problem that made him shy around other kids. "My thoughts just raced ahead of my tongue," Damon said. "I'd sing songs as therapy, and I got better, but I just kept quiet most of the time."

AT HOME ON THE DIAMOND

Soon he was letting his baseball bat do the talking. Johnny began to discover baseball and found he had a rare talent despite his young age. In his first year of T-ball, Johnny practically hit a home run every time he took a swing at the tee. Even before he started to play organized sports, Johnny had been a natural athlete. When he began to play soccer, he used his speed to dart across the field. But baseball was the sport that would eventually become a much bigger part of his life.

Although baseball came easy to him, finding the right equipment and instruction was not as simple. Born left-handed, Johnny was forced to use a right-handed glove that someone had given him because his family could not afford a

★ ★ ★ ★ ★

LOCAL BOY MAKES GOOD

Johnny Damon always liked growing up in Florida. His hometown, Orlando, had a great climate for an outdoors guy like Damon, with plenty of sun, warm weather, and outside distractions like Disney World to keep him and his friends occupied.

So it was extra special for Damon to be celebrated by the city of Orlando after the Red Sox won the World Series in 2004.

On November 11, 2004, Orlando held a parade for Damon along the city streets, with thousands of his fellow Orlando citizens lining the route to help him celebrate the Red Sox's world championship. The mayor declared it "Johnny Damon Day" in Orlando, and Damon was given a key to the city. The date was especially important to Damon. It was Veterans Day, and with Damon's father a 20-year veteran of military service, the day could not have gone any better.

"It is always great to be coming home, to a place where my dreams of becoming a baseball player started," Damon said in a press release announcing the celebration. "I want to thank the Mayor's Office and the Central Florida community for this recognition. Thank you for your support, and here is to believing in your dreams."

glove for him. As a consequence, he played his Little League games alternating between throwing hands. If he had to make a short throw, he went with his right hand; if he had to make a longer throw, he switched his glove and used his natural throwing arm. It was a good lesson for the young ballplayer—he learned to use all the talents and tools at his disposal to get the job done.

Johnny and his friends also received little coaching. They would often just experiment, taking advantage of the warm Florida climate to work on their skills all day most every day of the year.

Despite his disadvantages, Johnny showed promise as a Little Leaguer, at one point being selected second in his league draft ahead of players much older than he. The one boy who was picked above 8-year-old Johnny, for instance, was 12. In his first Little League season, Johnny hit above .300 while playing first base and even flashed a little bit of pitching ability with his nasty curveball.

Johnny was helped by the fact that he was used to playing against older competition. He often played ball with his older brother and his friends, which forced Johnny to keep up and play at a higher level than other kids his age. He was sometimes treated roughly, but he learned to think quickly and move even more quickly. Pretty soon he was hitting long home runs and gracefully running down line drives in center field—and catching them. Time and time again.

Because Johnny's parents were so busy working, they never pushed him into any particular activity. He had the freedom to choose the sports he enjoyed. He was not forced by his parents to play baseball; he just did it because he liked it. In fact, Johnny's father had little idea that his son was a good player at all, not realizing how talented he was until years later when scouts would come by to watch him in high school. "We both had two jobs," his father, Jimmy, said. "It wasn't until scouts started to call the house that I had any idea (how good Johnny was as a ballplayer). I just thought he could get a college education out of it."

In some ways, Johnny simply became used to his baseball skills. When he would play home-run derby with friends, he was surprised when he *didn't* hit a home run.

Johnny had grown into a player who was feared by opposing pitchers. Not only was he a good player, but he was also big for his age—6 feet tall (183 centimeters) and close to 180 pounds (82 kilograms) by the time he was 13. As good a hitter as Johnny was, he was also a terrific fielder and thrower. At age 13, while playing in a South Orange Little League play-off game against a team from the Dr. Phillips Little League, he showed just how good his arm was. After fielding a pop fly in center field, Johnny spied the other team's runner at third base heading for home. Almost immediately, he unleashed a laser dart of a throw to the third baseman that kept the astonished runner from tagging. He went on to throw out a few other runners in the game, as well.

Even though Damon would later gain a reputation in the major leagues as a soft-throwing outfielder, those Little League players who saw him that day would swear that Johnny had a cannon for an arm. Unfortunately, that cannon arm would never be the same after Johnny injured it a few years later in a sandlot football game and was forced to change his throwing motion.

Still, Johnny's all-around game made him a star wherever he played. In seventh grade, he tried out for the baseball team at Walker Junior High, a team that had never had a seventh-grade starter. The team's coach, though, was willing to make a deal with Johnny: if he was good enough to start, he would start, regardless of his age.

Luckily for that coach, Johnny did not waste the opportunity to wow teammates and opposing players that year, ripping line drives at the plate and snaring would-be hits like

While with the Red Sox, Johnny Damon made a throw back to the infield from his knees during a game in April 2005 against the Yankees. Damon's strengths as a center fielder—his speed and his ability to rob batters of hits—were evident even back when he was playing Little League.

flies. After making the team as a starter, he went on to finish the season second in hitting and earned a move from right field to center field, his preferred position.

A BROTHER'S GUIDANCE

After a while, however, baseball became less important to Johnny. He began to get into the wrong types of activities and spent more time with his friends. Eventually his brother, James, saw that Johnny could be getting himself into trouble and sat him down for a talk. James let him know that there were not too many Johnny Damons around and that he could play baseball in college and beyond if he wanted.

Johnny realized that his brother was right; he had a rare talent for the sport. Because of his brother, Johnny never did leave baseball.

When he was 14, Johnny entered his first year of high school at Dr. Phillips High School, where he discovered another of his talents: football. He eventually became good enough to make the varsity team in his second year, but he never loved the sport the way he loved baseball. For one thing, his coaches wanted him to be a safety on defense. Johnny instead had dreams of being a wide receiver, making over-the-shoulder catches and snapping cornerbacks at the knees with lightning-quick jukes and spins. When his coaches would not let him seek his stardom on offense, Johnny quit the team. Besides, he was playing baseball all year round by that time.

Of course, Johnny did not always get his way on the high school baseball team, either. Though he made the varsity squad in his first year, Johnny struggled initially, unable to harness the joy he felt when he played sandlot baseball as a kid and blasted homer after homer over his friends' heads. He was putting too much pressure on himself to succeed, and he stopped having fun. His coaches eventually sent him down to the junior-varsity team.

His next year proved to be a much better one, as he was back on the varsity team, which finished 22–8 but did not get far in the play-offs. The year after that, Johnny began to play on an even higher level. He was on the Central Florida All-Stars squad. Also on the team was one of his future teammates on the 2004 World Champion Red Sox, second baseman Mark Bellhorn (who would hit a memorable game-winning home run in the opener of the 2004 World Series against the St. Louis Cardinals). In fact, during his high school baseball career, Johnny would play with many talented young players who would end up joining him in the major leagues.

In his junior year, Johnny's dedication to baseball was once again put to the test. An avid runner who had starred on the Dr. Phillips track team, Johnny nonetheless had to choose between the two spring sports when his baseball games became more and more important to him. Though he once chose running over baseball in his freshman year, after he was demoted to the junior-varsity team, this time Johnny went with the sport he was destined to play. After all, Johnny did not have to look much farther than a baseball diamond to showcase his tremendous speed, scampering after fly balls in the outfield and stretching singles into scorching-fast doubles on the base paths.

Johnny also did plenty of running for his high school baseball coach, Danny Allie, who made sure his players hustled by timing them when they ran on and off the field. Coach Allie taught Johnny that it did not matter if he was darting into a headfirst slide at home plate or simply running out a grounder, he had to make the best effort he could. That lesson would stick with Johnny even when he made it to the majors, where he would become known as someone who could hit a home run, steal a base, and make a diving catch in the outfield all while playing on a painful broken foot.

Coach Allie's methods worked for his other players, too, and the team became one of the best in the country during Johnny's junior year. The team made it all the way to the semifinals of the state tournament and even had a three-run lead in the fourth inning of that game. Then, the opposing team's coach pointed out that Dr. Phillips' star pitcher was wearing a necklace and had to be disqualified from play according to the rules. Johnny's team went on to lose, a reversal of fortune that he would eventually suffer again when the Red Sox fell victim in 2003 to the come-from-behind Yankees. If Johnny learned anything his junior year, it was that he hated to lose.

After his junior-year season, Johnny once again was recruited to play on an all-star team that faced squads from across the country. This time, he was playing with two athletes who would go on to become some of the best hitters in major-league history: Alex Rodriguez and Todd Helton. Johnny excelled among the best players of his generation, scoring 19 runs and driving in 19 more runs in 10 games that summer.

Senior year had some ups and downs for Johnny. On the one hand, he was happy to reunite with the track team, which welcomed him back. And he continued to be a good student, receiving mostly A's in his classes. On the baseball field, however, he was facing heaps of pressure as the high school player one announcer called "the number-one player in the country" during one of Johnny's games.

He was named top schoolboy talent in the country by *Baseball America* in 1992, and *USA Today* named him to its High School All-America team. Johnny was also the Florida Gatorade Player of the Year.

By most players' standards, Johnny was indeed having a great year: He hit .305 and continued to play well in the outfield. Johnny's performance, though, fell short of his own expectations. It seemed that every crack of the bat, every screaming line drive over the shortstop's head would send the ball straight to a fielder's glove.

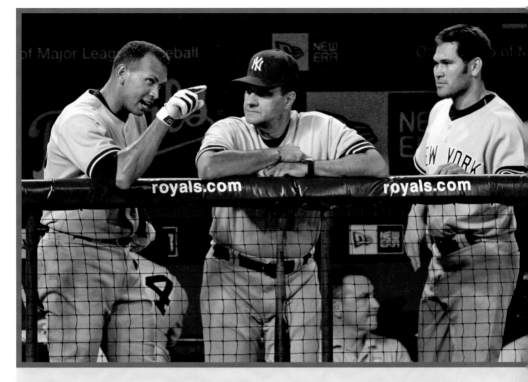

Alex Rodriguez *(left)* spoke with Yankees manager Joe Torre *(center)* and Johnny Damon during a game against the Kansas City Royals in July 2007. When Damon and Rodriguez were in high school, they played together on a summer all-star team.

As a result, he fell out of the first round of the 1992 amateur draft to become the thirty-fifth pick overall, by the Kansas City Royals.

As his brother had told him, however, Johnny would have a chance to play in college, as well. He received interest from many schools all over the country and was eventually given a scholarship to play baseball for the University of Florida. He was set to go, but being drafted made him weigh his options. He realized that his parents could use the money from a minor-league contract and that even a baseball scholarship was not going to be free. At the same time, Johnny was enticed by the chance to become an even bigger star in college, playing before bigger crowds and enjoying the life of a college student.

In the end, being drafted by Kansas City persuaded Johnny to skip college and go straight into professional baseball.

Johnny was more than satisfied with that. The Royals were a perfect fit for him—they were the team he had rooted for as a kid, because he was born in Kansas. The Royals' spring-training facility was also close to where Johnny's family lived in Florida.

Johnny Damon's prospects were looking up after high school. But life in the minor leagues was another challenge in the waiting.

Minor Leagues, Major Lessons

Johnny Damon knew that he had some serious baseball talent. In high school games, and even in some of his early minor-league games, he found himself genuinely surprised if he did not hit the ball hard on every swing. Plenty of times, he hit the ball plenty hard. Before the draft, the scouts had taken notice.

Yet on draft day, it occurred to Damon that there were a lot of other talented ballplayers out there, too. The Milwaukee Brewers and the Houston Astros had sent word along that they were very interested in drafting him, but neither team had been sure it wanted to use its first pick on Damon. Some scouts were comparing Damon to Barry Bonds and Ken Griffey, Jr., but Damon thought that his game was closer to that of Kirk Gibson, the Detroit Tiger and Los Angeles Dodger great who was more of a pure five-tool player: hit, hit for power, field, throw, and run. In Damon's eyes, he felt he could perform all of those skills well, although history would show that one weakness in Damon's game was his throwing arm. During his years in the big leagues, Damon was rarely at the top of the list in outfield assists—meaning he did not throw out a lot of runners on the base paths.

Taken by the Royals with their thirty-fifth pick, 18-year-old Johnny Damon realized that, by going professional, all the talk in the world was not going to help him. He needed to show the Royals—and all of baseball—what he could do on the field.

First, he had to attend to business.

PAY TO PLAY

One of the earliest highlights of Damon's minor-league career was getting paid to play baseball for the first time. He had always played for fun, and he was not quite sure what to expect at first as a high school graduate with little bargaining power to get himself a good deal.

Luckily for Damon, his brother stepped in again and helped track down sports agent Scott Boras, who handles the contracts of some of the biggest names in baseball. Boras had run into Damon once in high school, and he helped advise James Damon in negotiating a contract with the Royals. Damon eventually signed for a $250,000 bonus and a monthly salary of $800.

As a teenager growing up without much money, Damon viewed his first paycheck as if he had won the lottery. He used some of the money to buy his first car. And for the first time, Damon could say he was a professional baseball player.

His first chance to show that he deserved the money was in the Gulf Coast League, a Rookie league in which the teams played less than half the games that higher minor-league teams played. Damon was happy to be playing in Florida, not too far from his family, and his statistics showed his comfort—a sizzling .349 batting average and 23 stolen bases in 58 games.

The next spring, in 1993, Damon reported to camp with the Kansas City Royals' Class A ball club, the Rockford Royals, with whom he would play his first full minor-league season. He immediately realized that new recruits like him were not always welcomed by those teammates who were returning to the club. Some of those veterans saw him as a threat to their chances to move up to the big leagues. In many ways, it's tough to be a good teammate on a minor-league club; all the players want to win games, but they also want to play well for themselves so that they can advance to the next team in the farm system.

Damon was fortunate to have a coach in Rockford who would teach him how to deal with adversity. Coach Mike Jirschele had once been a minor-league player, but he was never good enough to make it to the major leagues. He made sure Damon realized that talent alone was not enough to get a good player to the next level; he needed to put in hard work and have an unbreakable will to win, too.

By then, Damon had already gained a reputation as Kansas City's next great player. Scouts believed that he could take the reins of the Royals and spark the team with his consistent hitting and sprinter's speed. Local sports reporters began to call him the next George Brett, the famous Royal who was just finishing up his career in Kansas City at the time. They even appeared in a commercial together when Damon was 20. For a young kid just out of high school, being compared to Brett, an all-time great who had once hit .390 in a season, could have been a reason to become a little arrogant. But Damon was not the only star in the minor leagues at the time.

Other players were also being touted as future greats. Just as he played with future Red Sox teammate Mark Bellhorn on his high school summer team, Damon was playing against minor-league players who would end up sitting next to him in the Boston dugout years later. Trot Nixon, who was playing for

George Brett of the Kansas City Royals watched as his home run left the park during a game in September 1980 against the Minnesota Twins. That season, Brett batted .390 and Kansas City won the American League pennant. As Johnny Damon made his way through the Royals' farm system, reporters deemed him the next George Brett.

the Lynchburg Red Sox, was a well-known player and great athlete who chose baseball over a chance to quarterback the North Carolina State University football team. Another future member of the 2004 world champion Red Sox, Bill Mueller, also often played against Damon's teams.

THE FIRST MAN UP

Despite adjusting to minor-league life and a new hitting position as the leadoff batter, Damon managed to have a promising year at the plate in his first season in Rockford. He hit .290 in 127 games, stole 59 bases, and was named the third-best prospect in the Midwest League.

That Damon had to become a much different hitter as a leadoff man made his statistics all the more impressive. Instead of aggressively swinging at the ball, he had to learn to take pitches at the beginning of the count to improve his chances to get on base. Years later, when Damon would conduct baseball camps for kids, he would emphasize the importance of taking pitches for the good of the team. Making a pitcher throw 10 to 12 pitches each at-bat would wear the pitcher out quickly. Then, the manager would have to replace him, usually with a pitcher of lesser caliber.

Considering his great athleticism and power at the plate, Damon had a hard time watching pitches go by that he would normally try to wallop into the grandstands.

"I was often told, 'Take the first pitch,'" Damon wrote in *Idiot: Beating "The Curse" and Enjoying the Game of Life.* "But very often the first pitch was the best pitch I was going to see. It's a problem I'm still wrestling with today."

Later on, Damon would develop the skill of fouling off pitches, which would allow him to swing the bat like he wanted to without striking out. When he was in the major leagues, Damon would awe fans as he fought off pitch after pitch, waiting for that juicy fastball across the plate that he could smoke into the gap for a standup double. Like most left-handed batters, Damon could also get to first base in a hurry, as the follow-through of his swing naturally pointed him in that direction.

WEDDING BELLS

At 19, Damon was also growing in other ways. That year, he married his high school sweetheart, Angie Vannice, whom he met in his freshman year. They dated throughout high school, and Damon and Vannice often would see each other between

Breaking his bat, Johnny Damon fouled off a ball against the Seattle Mariners in July 2004. As a leadoff hitter in the minor leagues, Damon learned to hit more foul balls, which makes the pitcher have to throw more pitches.

games when he began to play in the minor leagues. Life with a young minor-league ballplayer was not easy. Damon traveled a lot and, like many minor leaguers, moved from team to team. Starting the year in Rockport and ending it in Wichita, Kansas, or Midland, Texas, was a fact of life. People had to get used to it: players, wives, kids, other family members, and friends. That's the way it is in minor-league ball.

Damon understood that right away and thrived in his new environment. After a full season with the Rockford Royals, Damon moved to a higher Class A team in Wilmington, Delaware, in 1994. Once again, he showed he could play; he hit .316 and demonstrated some clutch hitting by knocking

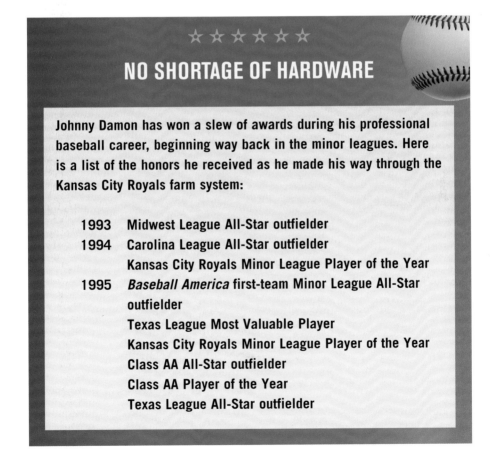

★ ★ ★ ★ ☆

NO SHORTAGE OF HARDWARE

Johnny Damon has won a slew of awards during his professional baseball career, beginning way back in the minor leagues. Here is a list of the honors he received as he made his way through the Kansas City Royals farm system:

1993	Midwest League All-Star outfielder
1994	Carolina League All-Star outfielder
	Kansas City Royals Minor League Player of the Year
1995	*Baseball America* first-team Minor League All-Star outfielder
	Texas League Most Valuable Player
	Kansas City Royals Minor League Player of the Year
	Class AA All-Star outfielder
	Class AA Player of the Year
	Texas League All-Star outfielder

in 75 runs in 119 games. His play garnered attention across the Carolina League. The league's managers named him best defensive outfielder, best hitting prospect, and most exciting player.

Thanks to his rapid improvement, Damon was promoted again the next season, this time to the Wichita Wranglers, a Class AA team in the Texas League. Once again, he proved he belonged by hitting a blistering .343 and swatting 16 home runs, more than twice the number he hit in his previous minor-league seasons.

Damon was quickly showing why so many scouts in the Kansas City organization had wanted him for their team. He could hit for average, had pop in his bat, could run the bases, and sucked up hits in center field like a Hoover vacuum cleaner. But even players as talented as Damon often had to wait years to get a chance to prove themselves on the big stage. In winning organizations like the New York Yankees, minor-league players often find themselves unable to make the jump to the big leagues, either because an excellent player is already at their position or because the team has enough money to buy an established player in the free-agency market.

THE CALL-UP

In Kansas City, however, Damon was fortunate enough to come along at a time when the team simply was not as a good as it had been in the previous decade, when it won the American League pennant in 1980 and the World Series in 1985. After his exceptional play for the Wranglers, Damon got the news every minor-league player dreams about: the call-up to the major leagues. The Royals needed an outfielder, and they did not want to wait any longer for their star to develop in the minors. Damon's coach actually played a little trick on him to let him know he had made the jump; he left the center fielder's name off the lineup for the day's game and purposely led him on when Damon questioned why he was not playing. Always a gamer, Damon could not figure out why he would be left off the roster.

When he finally realized what was happening, however, Damon was floored. Not only was he leaving his season in Class AA before it was finished, but he was also skipping Class AAA altogether. That day, he hopped on a plane headed to Kansas City and the major leagues.

4

Kansas City, Here I Come

At the time of Johnny Damon's call-up to the Kansas City Royals, the team's roster was going through a major shake-up. Veteran players, including former All-Star Vince Coleman, had been cut, and the organization was bringing in younger players like Damon from the minor leagues. The year was 1995, one year after the Royals had started to trade or cut the players that had once made them a formidable team in the American League. Kansas City was still in the pennant race when Damon came aboard mid-season, but the Royals were a team that would begin to slip out of the play-off picture as the 1990s progressed.

The pressure to perform came right away for the 21-year-old Damon. Before his first game, on August 12, Royals manager Bob Boone told him that he would be hitting leadoff—Damon was being thrown straight into the fire. The Royals were facing the Seattle Mariners, a team that was struggling at the time, much like Kansas City. Unlike the Royals, however, Seattle was on the upswing; the Mariners had young stars like Ken Griffey, Jr., and Randy Johnson and ended up making the play-offs that year thanks to a hot streak in September.

MAJOR-LEAGUE DEBUT

Though he was not facing the flame-throwing Johnson in his first major-league at-bat, Damon was still nervous. He was not in the minor leagues anymore; there were thousands of fans at Kauffman Stadium in Kansas City, all watching the new kid from Florida who came packaged as their next great star. Damon might as well have been under a microscope.

His first time up, Damon gripped his bat, glared at Seattle's pitcher, Tim Belcher, and dug in for his initial taste of big-league heat. He wanted to prove that he was the leadoff hitter that he and everyone in the organization believed he could be—the last thing he wanted to do was weakly send Belcher's first pitch into the mitt of one of Seattle's players. Though he did hold off, ultimately it did not matter; he popped out to end his first at-bat, and he did the same his second time up.

During his third at-bat, Damon would have better luck. He hit a grounder down the first-base line, usually an out. But Seattle's first baseman, Tino Martinez, was playing too far from the bag, and the ball rolled all the way into the outfield. His heart racing, Damon sped to first base and rounded the corner, understanding that he would have a chance for two. By the time the right fielder could scoop up the ball and hit the cutoff man, Damon was steaming across second and heading for third, his legs pumping furiously as the cheering crowd buzzed all around him.

Johnny Damon successfully stole second base as New York Yankees shortstop Randy Velarde leaped through the air to catch an errant throw during a game in August 1995. After being called up from the minors that month, Damon hit .282 in 47 games with the Royals.

As the throw came in, Damon slid into the bag and was ruled safe by the umpire; his first major-league hit was a rare triple.

Damon collected two more hits that night, finishing 3-for-5 in a game Kansas City would win. The rookie had served notice that he was as good as advertised, and the team began to respond as a result. When Damon first joined the Royals, they were 2½ games out of the lead for the wild-card play-off spot; a week later, they were up by 2½. The local press loved Damon's inspired play, and the fans were excited. In his first month as a major leaguer, Damon was electrifying the team—just as he had hoped.

As the season came to a close, Kansas City was not able to hold onto its wild-card lead, which eventually went to the New York Yankees. The Royals also could not keep up in the American League Central with the Cleveland Indians, who were enjoying one the finest seasons in the team's history and went on to play in the World Series that year. Though Damon finished the season with encouraging statistics—he hit .282 in 47 games—the Royals simply did not have enough great players to compete. The team had said goodbye to past stars like hitting great George Brett and Cy Young winner David Cone, and most of the younger players coming up would not be that good right away.

A TEAM IN FLUX

In 1996, Johnny Damon finished his first full year in the majors on a losing Royals team that had slashed even more of its payroll to save money. Kansas City was nowhere near being a competitive play-off team that year, winding up at the bottom of the American League Central with a record of 75–86. The team was willing to wait for its youngsters to develop, but it was paying the price.

"There was no money, and no veterans to help us greenhorns understand what we were going through," Damon wrote in *Idiot*. "We were just a bunch of kids who'd had success in the minor leagues, and it became a tinkering, learning process."

Damon compiled good stats for just a second-year player that season, but he was still learning. His .271 batting average was not necessarily going to ensure him a full-time slot in the batting order, and it was not even protection from being sent down to the minors again the following season.

Luckily for Damon, Kansas City's commitment to its youth movement meant that he would get a chance to play again on another struggling Royals team in 1997. Early on, he found himself the odd man out in the outfield, and he played infrequently as a result. When outfielder Jermaine Dye went down with an injury that spring, however, Damon was thrust

☆ ☆ ☆ ☆ ☆ ☆

THE KANSAS CITY ROYALS

When Johnny Damon joined the Kansas City Royals in 1995, the team was beginning a decline that continues to this day. Such struggles were not always the case for the Royals, who reached the top of their success a decade earlier.

The Royals made their debut in the 1969 season. The Athletics had played in the city from 1955 to 1967, when they left for Oakland. Major League Baseball, seeking to grow to 24 teams, granted Kansas City one of its four new expansion teams to begin play in 1969. The other teams were the Seattle Pilots (who moved to Milwaukee in 1970), the San Diego Padres, and the Montreal Expos (now the Washington Nationals). In their first season, the Royals finished 69–93, the best record among the four new teams.

By 1971, their third year in existence, the Royals had posted a winning record, 85–76, to finish second in the American League West. In the mid-1970s, the team formed a solid nucleus with players like George Brett and Frank White that would stay together for most of the next decade.

Beginning in 1976, the Royals won three consecutive American League West titles, but each year they lost to the back into the starting role he knew he was ready to fill. Because of his great speed and athleticism, he was also often used as a pinch runner and a late-inning defensive replacement in the games he did not start.

Damon, though, was not completely happy. After working so hard on his leadoff skills, he was finding himself scattered throughout the lineup during the season, not knowing if he was going to bat first or ninth on any given night. He

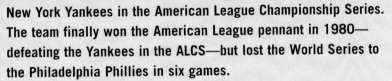

New York Yankees in the American League Championship Series. The team finally won the American League pennant in 1980—defeating the Yankees in the ALCS—but lost the World Series to the Philadelphia Phillies in six games.

Also in 1980, much of the baseball world was following the Royals to see if Brett would hit .400 for the season, a feat that was last accomplished by Ted Williams in 1941. He was batting .400 as late as September 19, but Brett ended up with a still-stellar .390 batting average for the year.

Over the next few years, the Royals finished first or second in the American League West until 1985, when they again played in the World Series. This time, they faced their cross-state rivals, the St. Louis Cardinals, in what was called the "I-70 Series"—named after the interstate that connects the two cities. Kansas City came back from a three-games-to-one deficit to win the Series, drubbing the Cardinals in the final game, 11-0.

The Royals continued to post winning records into the early 1990s but then sunk into a decline. Since 1995, Kansas City has had only one winning season—in 2003, when the team finished 83–79.

was having a hard enough time adjusting to the high level of play in the big leagues, and he found the lack of stability frustrating. As a result, he did not progress much from the year before, finishing with a similar batting average of .275.

By 1998, Damon and the Royals would enjoy a bit of an upswing, though the team was still going through growing pains. Damon had far more at-bats that year and secured himself a more reliable place in the Kansas City lineup. Again, his batting average was much like the past two seasons—.277. His statistics had not improved dramatically, but he was poised for a breakout year.

PROGRESS AT THE PLATE

That year came in 1999, when the Royals finally got some production out of their young stars. Besides Damon, future All-Stars Dye, Carlos Beltrán, and Mike Sweeney were providing pop to the lineup. Damon had his best season yet, finally crossing the .300 mark with a .307 batting average. He also hit 14 home runs and drove in a personal best 77 RBIs.

Unfortunately for the Royals, they were like many teams during baseball's long-ball era of the late 1990s; they had plenty of bats but few reliable arms. The team's pitching was especially flimsy in the bullpen, which surrendered lead after lead that Damon and his fellow position players helped build. Despite its outstanding offensive production, Kansas City would only win a paltry 64 games that year.

If Damon was discouraged, it did not show in his play, however; if 1999 was his breakout year, 2000 was the year he landed on fans' national radar. He was finally being considered a complete player, someone who could hit for power and average, and throw in some speed to boot. He finished the season with a stellar .327 average and drove in 88 RBIs—no easy task for a full-time leadoff hitter whose at-bats usually came with no one on base. He also led the league in stolen bases (46) and

Johnny Damon and Jermaine Dye celebrated after Damon scored the winning run in the twelfth inning of a game on June 10, 2000, between the Royals and the Pirates. Damon was beginning to make his mark in the game in the 1999 and 2000 seasons. He batted .327 in 2000, his best season ever.

runs scored (136) that year, further cementing his status as one of the game's most productive leadoff men.

Some of Damon's new confidence came from the Royals' manager, Tony Muser, who replaced Boone in 1997. Muser gave Damon a chance to anchor the team's outfield by playing center field full time, something he had not been able to do consistently until that point. By 2000, Damon also became the team's unquestioned leadoff hitter. In fact, the team as a whole played better in 2000, improving to 77 wins for the season.

Damon finally felt good about his role on the team, and even the Kansas City fans were beginning to come around after suffering through the team's last few seasons. At last, Damon did not have to feel like the new guy, the one taking the place of the local legend. Now he was the star, and his prospects were looking up.

Oakland
Calls

Johnny Damon's baseball life was good after the 2000 season—and getting better.

Damon was coming off a great year, and he and Angie were raising their young twins, Jaxson and Madelyn, who were born the year before. No longer the wide-eyed kid who was drafted straight out of high school, Damon was on course for the baseball greatness he had envisioned. The next few years, though, would show him that life was not always so easy.

During the off-season, Damon realized that his time was probably up in Kansas City, which was not going to be able to keep him around as his improving play demanded a more lucrative contract. The Royals were a small-market team, with fewer fans and fewer ways to make money than franchises like the Yankees and the Red Sox, which could rely on millions of fans coming to the park and watching games on television each year. When a young player like Damon became a star, Kansas City's management had to trade him away to get minor-league prospects or other players in return. If the organization waited too long, the player would leave as a free agent, and the Royals would get nothing.

That winter after the 2000 season, Damon's name came up in trade talks with numerous teams, including the Yankees, the New York Mets, and the Los Angeles Dodgers. One team that was not on his radar was the Oakland A's, which had quietly become a World Series contender thanks to smart player development and intelligent trades made by general manager Billy Beane. The team had surprised many by making the playoffs the year before, and the young pitching nucleus of Tim Hudson, Mark Mulder, and Barry Zito was quickly jelling into one of the league's best. Now Oakland was going after hitting to match its pitching, and Johnny Damon would be an ideal addition.

A TRADE IS MADE

In January 2001, Damon was vacationing in Hawaii when he learned that he had been traded to the A's. He welcomed the news at first, but moving away from Kansas City would not be so simply done. For one thing, the Damons had just bought a house in Orlando, Florida, and Angie Damon hoped to raise their twins there; she was not too happy about Damon going to Oakland. Being a ballplayer was already a tough job with the constant travel and long season, and Damon's move to the West Coast meant that he would be even farther from his family. Damon, though, realized that the stardom and riches of baseball came with consequences, and moving his life to Oakland would be one of them.

As it turned out, Oakland might not have been the best place to be a family man. The A's clubhouse had earned a reputation as one of the craziest and most free-spirited in the league. Unlike Kansas City, where the coaches focused on conditioning the young and raw players, Oakland was like a circus. The team's slugger, Jason Giambi, rode a Harley Davidson motorcycle, took teammates out for rowdy nights on the town, and was covered with tattoos. Zito charmed local reporters and fans with his laid-back, surfer persona and was nicknamed "Planet Zito" because of his spacey demeanor.

These eccentric individuals were the missing element in Kansas City; players like Giambi and Zito were talented on the field, but they also brought leadership and camaraderie to the clubhouse. It was the same energy that later helped the 2004 Boston Red Sox stay loose and unaffected as the team battled against "the Curse," which some fans believed could make even the greatest players buckle under the pressure.

Although the 2001 A's partied hard and shocked their fans, they also had confidence. Damon soon saw that this was a team that knew how to play the game and knew how to look good doing it.

FRONT-OFFICE VISIONARY

Just as important, they were overseen by a general manager with a grand vision. Beane, a former baseball player himself, was widely celebrated in some baseball-strategist circles as an early master of the science of sabermetrics. Like Kansas City, Oakland is a small-market team and has less revenue available when it comes to players' salaries. So instead of paying for the league's best players, as some teams did, Beane changed the way he looked at putting together a team. Instead of relying solely on old-fashioned scouting of players, he also placed strong emphasis on using the math-driven method of sabermetrics to explain why some players were good and others were not. For example, sabermetrics concludes that on-base percentage is a much more useful statistic to gauge a player's production than batting average, which only counts hits.

Sabermetrics was not initially accepted by older, more grizzled baseball analysts, but Beane's success in putting together an inexpensive A's team that could compete with powerhouses like the Yankees earned him accolades. While the A's were talented, however, they still could not win a World Series without a good leadoff man, which prompted Beane to trade for Kansas City's up-and-coming center fielder.

☆ ☆ ☆ ☆ ☆ ☆

A COLORFUL HISTORY

The Oakland A's team that Johnny Damon joined in 2001 was known for its eccentric players, like Jason Giambi and Barry Zito. Colorful characters, though, are nothing new to the A's, and perhaps the most colorful was Charlie Finley, the owner of the team in the 1960s and the 1970s.

In the 1970s, he had the A's wear solid green or solid gold jerseys, similar to the uniforms worn by amateur softball teams. At the time, other major-league teams wore all-white uniforms at home and all-gray ones on the road. One season, in conjunction with a Mustache Day promotion, Finley offered $500 to any player who grew a mustache. Every player grew one, helping to define the look of the team. Most ball clubs back then banned facial hair. Finley tried orange baseballs in a few spring-training games, and on Opening Day in 1970, he trotted out yellow bases, which were soon banned by Major League Baseball.

Besides these eccentricities, Finley was also known for bigger controversies. When the A's were in Kansas City and Oakland, Finley continually sought to move the team to other

"We're ecstatic," Beane said in an article just after the trade was completed. "Damon is a premier leadoff guy. It adds dimension. We're a more complete team. We're a better team. At least on paper, we like what we have done relative to the rest of the division."

To a visionary like Beane, Damon seemed to fit perfectly with what the A's were doing. Like other Oakland players, he had a good eye at the plate and could foul off pitches at will, which helped drive up a pitcher's pitch count and wear him out early. In reality, though, Damon suffered at the plate that

☆ ☆ ☆ ☆ ☆ ☆

cities. After Reggie Jackson hit 47 home runs in 1969, Finley threatened to send Jackson back to the minor leagues during a contract dispute. He did the same to Vida Blue after the pitcher won the Cy Young Award.

Years later, the A's players from the 1970s said they performed so well because they all despised Finley. The A's won three straight World Series titles, from 1972 to 1974, and then lost the 1975 American League Championship Series to the Boston Red Sox. After that season, Finley began to dismantle the club, trading some players and losing others to free agency. In 1979, just five years after winning their last World Series, the A's finished with a dreadful 54–108 record. In one game that year against the Mariners, they drew only 653 fans.

The Finley era, though, was about to come to a close. The following year, divorce proceedings forced Finley to sell the team. The A's were purchased by a local owner, Walter A. Haas, Jr., president of Levi Strauss & Co., who set about to change the team's image.

During an August 2001 game in Detroit, Johnny Damon paused to watch his three-run homer in the ninth inning. The blast gave the A's the win, 6-3. Damon had a so-so season at the plate, but Oakland had a much better year—winning 102 games and making the play-offs.

spring. He managed to improve a little later that summer, but statistically 2001 was one of the worst seasons of his career. He finished with a .256 batting average and only 49 RBIs.

Aside from Damon's poor hitting performance, the A's were still having a great year, however. Giambi was socking the ball all over the place, and Zito was freezing hitters with his zany, arcing curveball. The A's scared other teams; they were not just good, they were dangerous. The lineup was stocked with smart, clutch hitters, and the "Big Three," as Zito, Mulder, and Hudson were called, were making opposing teams look foolish at the plate. Despite his teammates' success, Damon never felt the ax fall; Oakland's manager, Art Howe, stuck with his leadoff man all year, letting him play through his struggles instead of benching him.

TO THE PLAY-OFFS FINALLY

The A's went on to win 102 games that year in a competitive American League. Many analysts were picking them to go all the way, despite the looming presence of the Seattle Mariners, which had won a record 116 games that season, and the New York Yankees, the team that had ruled baseball with four World Series titles in the last five years. For Damon, it was an exciting time, his first chance to be on a play-off team. It did not matter that his own statistics were unspectacular; playing team baseball was well worth it.

"At Oakland I really started to learn what it is to play the game of baseball," Damon said in *Idiot.* "I've always been a team player, but I really learned how important it is to give yourself up, take pitches so your teammates can see everything the pitcher might have that day. It's that unselfishness that helped me earn the respect of my teammates."

Oakland entered the play-offs via the wild card, finishing several games back in the American League West to the Seattle Mariners. The A's were matched against the American League East champs, the Yankees, in the divisional round.

Normally, such a matchup would paint the A's as the likable underdog, the small-budget David to the Yankee Empire's Goliath. This year, however, was one that had changed everyone's attitude toward the Bronx Bombers, who were now seen as the sentimental favorites. The terrorist attacks on September 11 had left New York's iconic Twin Towers in ruins, and the city was still picking up the pieces when play-off time rolled around.

Apart from the drama and emotion, though, many members of the A's believed that they were the better team. The first game, a duel between Oakland's Mulder and New York's Roger Clemens, seemed to prove them right, as the A's won 5-3. Leaving behind his regular-season frustrations, Damon had a monster game, going 3-for-3 and scoring a crucial run on a Giambi hit. If Damon felt the bright lights of play-off baseball bearing down on him, he did not show it.

Damon again excelled in the next game, another win for the A's, 2-0. Buoyed by the impeccable control of Hudson on the mound, the A's capitalized on the few mistakes the Yankees made, and Damon added the insurance run late in the game after he got on base with a triple. Up two games on the once-indomitable Yankees, Oakland had shocked the baseball world. The clowns of the American League West were giving the 2000 champs all they could handle, and the A's were going back to Oakland with their staff ace, Zito, set to take the mound.

JUST A WIN AWAY

Damon and the A's were one game away from advancing to the American League Championship Series. But like the heavyweight knocked to the mat with an early sucker punch, New York got up and brushed itself off. The real fight was about to begin. Game 3 was even more tense than the game before it, as the Yankees took a slim one-run lead into the bottom of the seventh inning. The A's were poised to score that inning, starting with a single from Jeremy Giambi, Jason's

Johnny Damon high-fived an Oakland A's bat boy after he scored the insurance run in the ninth inning of Game 2 of the 2001 American League Division Series. Damon had hit a triple to get on base. The A's beat the Yankees in the game, 2-0. Damon was appearing in the post-season for the first time in his career.

brother, to get on with two outs. The next batter, Terrence Long, tagged a shot down the right-field line for a double, and Giambi was heading toward home as the Athletics' third-base coach waved him around. Unfortunately for Oakland, the events that followed would not herald a new era of dominance by the A's but instead would add to the lengthy highlight reel of miraculous Yankee plays that defined the epic history of the Bronx Bombers.

New York's right fielder, Shane Spencer, zipped the ball in to cutoff man Alfonso Soriano. The ball got by Soriano, however, and also past first baseman Tino Martinez. Perhaps with any other team, the ball would have rolled harmlessly into the infield, and Giambi would have scored. The Yankees, though, were not any team. The ball was scooped up by shortstop Derek Jeter, who was way out of position along the first-base line, and almost instantaneously flipped to the catcher, Jorge Posada, who laid the tag on the dumbfounded Giambi as he loped to the plate. Giambi had not even bothered to slide, sure that there was no way Spencer's throw would reach home in time. The seemingly botched play ended up stifling the Athletics' only scoring opportunity, and they went on to lose the game 1-0.

The shift in momentum caused by that play ultimately proved too insurmountable even for the carefree A's. They handily lost the next game, 9-2, and the rubber game also went to the Yankees, 5-3. Just like that, the Athletics' 2001 party was snuffed out. And for Johnny Damon, who would become a free agent after the season, it was the last time he would ever wear an Oakland uniform.

"After the game I went up to Art Howe and said, 'Thank you,'" Damon wrote in *Idiot*. "I shed a tear or two, because I knew we'd had a magical year in Oakland, and now it was time for me to move on."

6

Life with the Red Sox

A few days after Christmas 2001, Dan Duquette, who was then the Red Sox general manager, was accosted by an excited young woman in a local restaurant.

"You're Dan Duquette!" the woman shouted.

"'Do I know you?" a startled Duquette replied.

"'No," she said, "but thank you, thank you, thank you for signing Johnny Damon!"

"That was the first hint I had," Duquette later said, "of how popular Johnny Damon was going to be."

In baseball numbers, the Red Sox got a bargain for a strapping leadoff hitter, center fielder, and swift base stealer. The numbers? A four-year deal worth $31 million. During the same period, the Red Sox were paying pitching ace Pedro Martínez $14 million a year and slugging, if sometimes

scatter-brained, left fielder Manny Ramírez $18 million annually.

THE FACE OF THE RED SOX

But it was not just what Damon could do on the field that would pay dividends for the BoSox. With matinee good looks, a sunny persona, and a gift of gab that played well with legions of adoring Red Sox fans, Damon immediately became an ambassador of goodwill for Red Sox Nation's ever-expanding fan base. More so, the signing gave the Red Sox a much-needed public face, a movie star in a blue cap with a red "B" on the front. The Yankees had Derek Jeter, the Cubs had Sammy Sosa, and the Braves had the Jones boys—Andruw and Chipper.

In the next few years, Damon became one of the most celebrated figures in Boston sports history. His face was everywhere: the film *Fever Pitch*; on TV shows like *Cribs*, *Celebrity Poker*, *Queer Eye for the Straight Guy*, *Saturday Night Live*, *Today*, and *Live with Regis and Kelly*; on the talk shows of David Letterman, Jay Leno, and Conan O'Brien; at book signings for his *Idiot: Beating "The Curse" and Enjoying the Game of Life*; in commercials for Puma, Dunkin' Donuts, Sprint, and DHL; on the covers of *Entertainment Weekly*, *Sports Illustrated*, and *Sports Illustrated for Kids*; inside a Daytona 500 pace car; even at Johnny Damon Day in Orlando.

Until Damon came along, the Red Sox had nobody like Jeter or Sosa—someone whose popularity transcended the game. Sure, Ramírez was a feared slugger, but he rarely talked to the press. And while Martínez was one of the greatest pitchers in the game, his moody demeanor and frequent spats with the Boston media made him somewhat reluctant to be the front man for the Red Sox.

Being a leader of Red Sox Nation was no small task. Over the past 10 years or so, the Red Sox have become, along with the Yankees, one of baseball's most popular teams. With Red

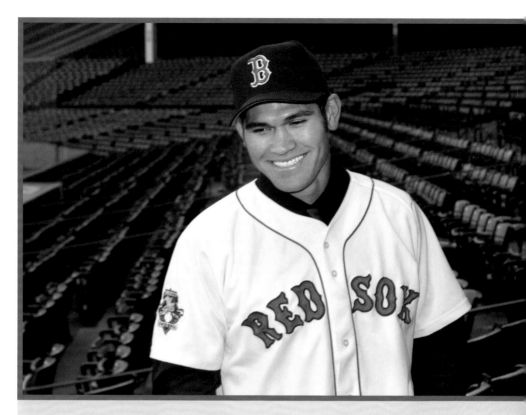

During a news conference in December 2001 to announce his signing by Boston, Johnny Damon modeled his new Red Sox jersey. He signed a four-year, $31 million deal with Boston. Before his arrival, the Red Sox had been an aloof team whose players had always seemed on edge. Damon, though, enjoyed the limelight.

Sox tickets at Fenway Park increasingly tougher to get (through 2007, the Sox had 388 consecutive sellouts), legions of fans took to the road to see the Sox in places like Baltimore, Tampa Bay, Toronto, and even West Coast ballparks in Anaheim and Seattle.

Recent Boston players have marveled at being in a tight game in Baltimore or Seattle and hearing the "home team" fans rise up and raise their voices in support of the Red Sox.

In many instances, Red Sox road games became de facto home games, with half the crowd in visiting cities rooting for the Red Sox.

Consequently, life with the revamped Red Sox was a real roller-coaster ride for the players. Make no mistake, many players did not want or need the pressure. You had to have a

★ ★ ★ ★ ☆

BOSTON, YOU'RE MY HOME

One reason Johnny Damon liked to play baseball in Boston was that it was a great sports town—maybe the best sports town in the United States.

Year in and year out, Boston's rabid sports base follow the region's four professional teams—the Red Sox, the Patriots, the Celtics, and the Bruins—with an intensity that is tough to match. Big-time college athletic programs like Boston College and the University of Massachusetts also add to the electricity in the region.

Having grown up in a city like Orlando, Florida, which had no professional sports team when he was a youngster and no college teams of note, Damon got a big kick out of the sports vibe that seemed to electrify Boston.

In fact, in one local publication's "Top Ten Sports Stories of 2001," the signing of Johnny Damon made the list (at No. 9). This was in a year in which the Patriots were headed to victory in the Super Bowl, the Celtics competed for the NBA championship, and the Bruins fought for a Stanley Cup. In Boston, the signing of a big-time ballplayer is a headline story.

With such a passionate sports following, there was no way a guy like Johnny Damon, who enjoyed the limelight, would fail in Boston.

thick skin to play in a city where generations of fans grew up under the common refrain that "baseball wasn't life or death, but the Red Sox were."

Johnny Damon knew he would thrive under the pressure. The money alone made him financially set for life. That meant a lot to Damon, who had earned only $800 a month as a minor-league ballplayer and had to moonlight as a construction-site surveyor to make ends meet. That was commonplace for young ballplayers like Damon, guys who were married and had young families to feed. The $31 million that the Red Sox gave Damon made him feel a sense of loyalty to the club and compelled him to get out there and grip and grin with the adoring public. Win or lose, Damon was always great with the fans, especially the kids, and he made plenty of time to participate in charity events and pitch in for a good cause.

His six years with the Royals and his year with the A's were rewarding for Damon, but for a guy who thrived in the spotlight, a big stage like Boston would really provide a challenge that, in the end, Damon just could not pass up.

A TEAM ON EDGE

What Damon found when he arrived in the Red Sox spring-training facility in Fort Myers, Florida, were the last gasps of a team that had feuded more within itself than with other teams. Damon recalls feeling that the players were anxious and on edge—not a good environment for a ball club looking to do some damage in the American League East. The team's ownership and management were famous for squabbling with the press and for signing washed-up players to big contracts. The farm system—the minor-league programs that major-league clubs use to groom young players—was neglected in Boston. Almost immediately after Damon arrived on the scene, the team was sold, and the club's general manager, Duquette, and manager, Joe Kerrigan, were shown the door.

The legendary love and support that the Red Sox fans showed their team was sorely being tested. To Damon's relief, the new owners, commodities trader John Henry and Hollywood television producer Tom Werner, were a breath of fresh air, hosting team parties on Henry's yacht and encouraging players to mingle with fans and engage the community at charity events and other public appearances.

Virtually overnight, the atmosphere in the Red Sox clubhouse loosened up. Damon took it upon himself to take players out to dinner at night. The Red Sox routine had long been that the players stayed holed up in their hotel rooms, ordering room service and avoiding the spotlight. Such an atmosphere was not what Damon had been used to in Oakland and Kansas City. Maybe it was because the pressure was so much greater in Boston, but, for one reason or another, the Red Sox did not hang out much together. For years, the joke in the Boston press in describing the Red Sox was "25 players, 25 cabs"—meaning that each player went his own way after a game instead of socializing with the guys.

A QUICK START

With a newfound camaraderie among the players, the Red Sox took off in 2002, winning 40 of their first 57 games. Damon was doing great—by the All-Star break in July, he had scored 66 runs and stolen 22 bases. Damon was batting .308. The Yankees were playing great ball, too, and the two teams were running neck and neck into the midseason.

To Damon, the Red Sox were in a great spot—tied or near the top and well-positioned to take the American League East and do some damage in the play-offs come fall. What he could not understand was the relentless negativity of the local media. In Boston, players had often said that sportswriters sharpened their teeth on the ankles of Red Sox players. Damon had long ago learned that it was useless to pay attention to the local media—the sportswriters did not know the players nearly as well as Damon did. Instead, Damon would relax and unwind with ESPN's *SportsCenter* or by reading the more straightforward accounts of games in *USA Today*.

The team cooled off a bit, entering the dog days of August playing .500 ball. Damon told his teammates after a clubhouse meeting that he would lead them to the play-offs. "And sure enough, that day I went out and hit the crap out of the ball," he said in *Idiot*. "In my mind—and I have a strong mind— I thought, we are going to the play-offs."

Still fairly new to Boston, Damon had not known much about the Curse of the Bambino. The legend goes that the Red Sox had been under a curse ever since owner Harry Frazee sold Babe Ruth to the New York Yankees after the 1919 season. What could not be denied was that the Red Sox had failed to win the World Series after Ruth went to the hated Yankees. After acquiring Ruth, the Bronx Bombers went on to win 26 titles over the next eight decades—far more than any other team in baseball.

If Damon did not know much about the Curse, though, he soon found out. In one game late in the season, when diving back to first base after an opposing pitcher tried to pick him off, Damon jammed his finger into the bag, dislocating it badly. Damon tried to play through the injury, but he knew his game would be affected for the rest of the year.

Although the Red Sox won 93 games, it was not enough to make the play-offs. They finished in second place in the American League East, 10½ games behind the Yankees. The Anaheim Angels, with a record of 99–63, beat out the Sox for the wild-card spot. Failure again filled the air outside of Fenway Park, and Damon had had enough of it.

He knew the Red Sox could beat the Curse and win the big one. Surely, Damon had done his part. He hit .286 for the year, scoring a whopping 118 runs, with 14 home runs,

After dislocating a finger during a pick-off attempt, Johnny Damon left the field with Red Sox trainer Jim Rowe *(center)* and manager Grady Little. Damon suffered the injury on August 22, 2002, in the first inning of a game against the Texas Rangers. Damon tried to play through the injury, but it hampered his game for the rest of the season.

34 doubles, and 11 triples out of the leadoff spot. He stole 31 bases, tops for the club. Damon was also the starting center fielder for the American League All-Star team, finishing only behind Seattle's popular Ichiro Suzuki in the fan voting. But it wasn't enough—Damon knew that he would have to do better.

Eight months earlier, Johnny Damon had sought to turn failure into success—and to assure Red Sox Nation that the players had the same high expectations that the fans had. At his first news conference, Damon had made a brash—but accurate—prediction. "When we win a World Series," he said, "we're going to be put on a pedestal and be immortalized forever."

It would take two more years, but Johnny Damon would prove to be a prophet yet.

Heartbreak and Headaches

The Red Sox, now stocked with marquee talent like Johnny Damon, David Ortiz, Manny Ramírez, Nomar Garcia-parra, and Pedro Martínez, were poised to make a big move in 2003—and make a big move they did.

The Sox and Damon played a memorable game against the Florida Marlins on June 27. Damon tied a major-league record by getting three base hits in the first inning of a 25-8 pummeling of the Marlins. The Red Sox scored 14 runs in that inning, 10 runs before a single out was recorded. In that first inning, Damon hit a single, a double, and a triple. He missed out on hitting for the cycle in the game, but he did bat 5-for-7.

Still, by late July, the Yankees were in front of the Red Sox, holding a four-game lead in the American League East. That did not worry Damon or the Red Sox. In mid-August, though,

The scoreboard on the Green Monster at Fenway Park showed the monster of a game the Red Sox played against the Florida Marlins on June 27, 2003. In the first inning, when the Sox scored 14 runs, Johnny Damon hit a single, a double, and a triple. He went 5-for-7 in the game.

the Sox lost two out of three in Seattle and then lost the first two back at home in the late innings against the A's. The fans of Red Sox Nation were beginning to lose their patience. After all, hadn't the Red Sox wilted in the summer heat before? Hadn't they blown golden opportunities to win championships in the past?

CURSED FOR SO MANY YEARS

Longtime Red Sox fans recall 1946, when the St. Louis Cardinals stole Game 7 of the World Series—and the championship banner itself. In the eighth inning, with the score tied 3-3, the

Cardinals' Enos Slaughter opened the inning with a single but was still stranded on first base with two outs. Then Cardinal slugger Harry "The Hat" Walker hit a line drive over Red Sox shortstop Johnny Pesky's head into left-center field. As Leon Culberson chased the ball down, Slaughter started his famous "Mad Dash" into baseball history. Pesky caught the throw from Culberson, turned and—astonished to see Slaughter headed for the plate—hesitated a split second before throwing home. Red Sox catcher Roy Partee needed to take a few steps up the third-base line to catch Pesky's throw, and Slaughter was safe at the plate. The Cardinals won the game and the Series, giving them their sixth championship. Red Sox fans could only shake their heads and wonder if the result would have been different if Boston superstar Ted Williams, who played hurt during the Series, was healthy and hitting like his usual self.

Two years later, the Red Sox suffered another autumn blow, losing a winner-take-all play-off game to the Cleveland Indians, who would go on to win the 1948 World Series and end a championship drought of their own.

In the 1950s and much of the '60s, with the exception of the remarkable Ted Williams and his successor in left field, Hall of Famer Carl Yastrzemski, the Red Sox remained mired in mediocrity, if not downright failure. The Red Sox would not return to the World Series until 1967, when they again faced the Cardinals. St. Louis had some weapons of its own in powerful pitcher Bob Gibson and prolific hitters Lou Brock and Curt Flood. The Series was close, but the Cardinals won that one, too, in seven games.

MORE DEVASTATING LOSSES

The Red Sox would return to the World Series in 1975 and 1986—only to lose in the most excruciating manner possible.

In 1975, in what ESPN described as the second-most-exciting World Series ever played, the Red Sox battled the Cincinnati Reds.

The sixth game of the Series was a 12-inning classic at Fenway Park, with TV sets tuned in long after most kids' bedtimes. Historic and memorable performances dominated the game: Red Sox pinch hitter Bernie Carbo getting a game-tying home run in the eighth; Reds reliever Will McEnaney pitching out of a bases-loaded, no-out jam in the bottom of the ninth; and Boston's Dwight Evans making a spectacular eleventh-inning catch to rob the Reds' Joe Morgan of a go-ahead home run. But the capper was Red Sox catcher Carlton Fisk's walk-off home run in the bottom of the twelfth inning. Fisk's home run gave the Sox a 7-6 win to send the Series to a deciding seventh game, which the "Big Red Machine" won on a ninth-inning single by Morgan to clinch the first of back-to-back World Series championships.

A devastating play-off loss to the Yankees in 1978 poured more salt into Red Sox Nation's wounds, as New York came from behind on Bucky Dent's three-run home run to beat the Sox 5-4. The Bronx Bombers would go on to beat the Los Angeles Dodgers in the World Series that year.

But it was 1986 that cemented the Red Sox's unfortunate reputation as one of the biggest all-time chokers in the history of baseball, if not all of sports.

The National League champion New York Mets had swaggered into the World Series as huge favorites, having won 108 games during the regular season. But the Amazin' Mets, as the New York fans called them, ran into a buzz saw in Games 1 and 2, both going to the underdog Red Sox.

In the first game at Shea Stadium in New York, Red Sox starter Bruce Hurst pitched eight scoreless innings, and Boston took the opener 1-0 on an unearned run. Game 2 matched 1985 National League Cy Young Award winner Dwight Gooden against 1986 American League Cy Young winner Roger Clemens, but neither ace lasted more than five innings. Boston's bullpen proved stronger than New York's; the Sox took a two-games-to-none edge with a convincing 9-3 victory, and the Series shifted to Fenway Park. Undaunted, the Mets got on the board with a 7-1 decision in Game 3, thanks to four runs in the first inning and seven strong frames from starter Bob Ojeda (who had pitched for Boston in 1985).

The Mets also grabbed Game 4. Catcher Gary Carter pounded a pair of home runs, Lenny Dykstra homered off the glove of Sox right fielder Dwight Evans, and the Mets cruised, 6-2. In Game 5, though, Bruce Hurst was back to flummox New York, beating back the Mets and their staff ace Gooden by a score of 4-2. Only one win away from their first World Series championship since 1918, the Red Sox had their ace, Clemens, on the hill in Game 6, and he found himself in a tight duel against Ojeda.

After nine innings, the game was deadlocked, 3-3. Boston's Dave Henderson led off the tenth inning with a home run, and a few minutes later Wade Boggs scored on Marty Barrett's single to give the Sox a 5-3 lead.

The Curse of the Bambino, 68 years in the making, was about to be banished, especially when hard-throwing Red Sox relief pitcher Calvin Schiraldi retired the first two Met hitters in the bottom of the tenth. With champagne corks about to pop from New Haven, Connecticut, to Kennebunkport, Maine, the Mets slapped three straight singles, and it was 5-4. Sox manager John McNamara summoned Bob Stanley from the bullpen, and Stanley promptly threw a wild pitch that tied the game. Then, on a full count, Mookie Wilson grounded a ball right to first baseman Bill Buckner. And in a scene that will never be forgotten by Fenway faithful, the ball scooted straight through Buckner's legs while Ray Knight scored the winning run.

Demoralized or not, the Red Sox grabbed a 3-0 lead in the second inning of Game 7, thanks in part to a pair of solo homers from Dwight Evans and Rich Gedman. The Mets came back and tied the game with three runs in the sixth, and went ahead for good with three more in the seventh off Schiraldi.

Red Sox first baseman Bill Buckner let a ground ball scoot through his legs in the tenth inning of Game 6 of the 1986 World Series, allowing the Mets to win the game. The Mets took the next game, too, to win the Series—one of many heartbreaking Red Sox losses over the years that contributed to the legend of The Curse of the Bambino.

Mets lefty Jesse Orosco finished off the Sox with two perfect innings of relief, and the Mets were champions.

All across New England, champagne corks remained unpopped and grown men cried as their beloved Red Sox had once again snatched defeat from the jaws of victory. If baseball defined Boston, as many of the city's denizens insisted it did, then failure—at the most critical times—defined the Red Sox. And had for decades.

SHAKING OFF THE PAST

Sixteen years would pass from the Red Sox nightmare in Shea Stadium before Johnny Damon signed with the Red Sox, and the heavy shadow of Boston's past failures seemed to haunt every nook and cranny of Red Sox Nation.

So with the Red Sox scuffling in August 2003, Damon, along with teammate and clubhouse mayor Kevin Millar, took matters into their own hands in an effort to revive the Sox's fortunes against the hated Yankees.

After the second brutal loss to Oakland, Millar stood up in the Red Sox clubhouse and told both the fans and the ever-negative Boston press to stop whining about the past and to let the 2003 Red Sox stand on their own, without the heavy anchor of earlier misfortunes weighing them down. "I want to see somebody cowboy up and stand behind this team and quit worrying about the negative stuff and last year's team, and the 1986 team and ten years ago," Millar told the Boston press gathered in the locker room. "I'm here to have fun. The past makes zero sense to me."

Damon and his teammates latched onto the boisterous Millar's catchphrase "Cowboy Up" and used it as a springboard to victory after victory in late 2003. In early September, the Sox took two straight from the Yankees, right there in Yankee Stadium.

The fans and the Boston press began to rally around the Red Sox, a fact that amused Damon. "The press is very knowledgeable, but their mood swings were a big distraction," he said. "One week we're getting it with both barrels . . . and the next week we're the darlings of the town."

It would be more "darlings" and less "barrels" the rest of the way into the play-offs, with Boston beating back the Mariners for the wild-card spot in the American League. That meant a date with Damon's old team, the Oakland A's, in the American League Division Series. Oakland was loaded with

"The past makes zero sense to me," Kevin Millar said in the Red Sox clubhouse after a series of losses in August 2003. He told the press and the fans to quit worrying about the Curse and let the Red Sox play. Millar's remarks spurred the team into the play-offs.

young talent like hurlers Barry Zito and Tim Hudson and hitters Miguel Tejada and Scott Hatteberg.

FIRST ROUND VS. THE A'S

A surprise bases-loaded, walk-off bunt by A's catcher Ramón Hernández clinched Game 1 for the A's in the twelfth inning, and Zito hurled a masterpiece for Oakland in Game 2. Before they were even in it, Damon and the Red Sox were well aware that they were almost out of the championship chase—if something good did not happen, and fast.

Something good did happen back home at "Friendly Fenway," where the BoSox grabbed Games 3 and 4 in exciting fashion. For luck, Damon's rowdy teammates decided to shave their heads, although Damon did not go along because he wanted to look good for the girls in the off-season. (Johnny and Angie Damon had decided to get a divorce in 2002.) "If I cut my hair off," he told Millar, "it might never grow back."

The ploy worked in Game 3, when the newly clean-shaven Trot Nixon hit a home run in the eleventh inning to win the game. Game 4 was equally close. With the Sox down 4-3 in the eighth inning, David Ortiz walloped a double into the right-field corner, scoring two key runs and icing the game for the Red Sox.

Now, with one game remaining in the series, it was back to Oakland in another of Boston's long line of "winner-take-all" games. As history shows, the Red Sox had not demonstrated a great track record in big games. And now they were faced with one of the biggest games in franchise history.

Damon knew his old teammates from his days in Oakland, and he knew they were deflated after having two gut-wrenching losses in a row back in Boston. The last thing Oakland wanted to do was get back on a plane to fly 3,000 miles (4,828 kilometers) and take on a suddenly rejuvenated Red Sox team in Game 5.

In a stroke of luck—and mismanagement on the part of the A's—the Oakland ballplayers had to wait around after Game 4 in Boston because their bags and gear were earmarked for a trip to New York and a date with the Yankees in the American League Championship Series. It had never occurred to A's management that the team could lose two games in Boston, and their overconfidence cost them. Now, with the tired A's waiting around for the bags to show up for a flight

★ ☆ ★ ☆ ★

DAMON'S
UNUSUAL WORKOUT REGIMEN

As a youngster, Johnny Damon did not always have the sturdy build and solid muscles he has today.

To bulk up during his formative years, Johnny would time himself as he climbed trees in his neighborhood. He told David Letterman on late-night television that he would "run up a tree as fast as [he] could." He also said that he would stay in the tree until people began to miss him.

To increase the speed he would need to steal bases and rob hitters of extra-base hits in center field, Johnny often raced against cars down his block as a teenager. Damon told a Providence newspaper in 2004: "I lived on a street (in the Orlando area) where the speed limit is 25 miles an hour, and the police enforce it. At night, I'd wait out there and when a car came by I would race the car home, so I think I can go at least 25 miles an hour. I scared some of the people, seeing a caveman racing after cars."

It is worth noting that the fastest world-class sprinters reach speeds of 27 to 28 miles per hour (43 to 45 kilometers per hour). That puts Damon in some very fast company.

back to Oakland, the Red Sox were already there, resting comfortably for the game the following night.

Game 5 started slowly, Damon recalled, like two prize fighters measuring each other up before the real blows started to fly. Manny Ramírez hit a huge three-run homer in the sixth inning to give the Sox a 4-1 lead. Oakland put two men in scoring position with one out in the ninth, and the Sox did not clinch until Derek Lowe fanned pinch hitter Terrence Long with the bases loaded and two out. Long was Lowe's second strikeout victim—both looking—in the nail-biting ninth.

Damon was having a quiet night at the plate and in the field until the seventh inning, when a short fly ball hit by Jermaine Dye to center field saw both Damon and second baseman Damian Jackson sprinting to the ball. With neither ballplayer aware that the other was coming, a sickening head-to-head collision occurred.

Both players lay still on the outfield grass after the crash, but it was soon clear that Damon's injury was more serious.

Jackson walked off the field without assistance, but Damon lay motionless for a full five minutes. Fearing the worst, medics ran out and Damon was placed in a neck brace, strapped to a stretcher, and wheeled off in an ambulance. Damon, who had suffered a concussion, was taken to Highland General Hospital for evaluation.

His recollection of the collision, even years later, remains cloudy. Teammates told reporters that, when he came to, Damon was completely disoriented, believing that he was still playing for his old team, the Oakland Athletics. Even weeks afterward, Damon continued to suffer blackouts and memory loss (all he could remember thinking was that Dye's pop-up would be an "easy catch"). He told his Red Sox teammates that he only had a vague recollection of the first two games of the ensuing 2003 play-off series against the Yankees (he sat out both games), and he said that his memory of Game 3, in

Johnny Damon and Damian Jackson brutally collided while trying to field a fly ball during Game 5 of the 2003 American League Division Series against the Oakland A's. Damon, who suffered a concussion, lay unconscious on the field for five minutes.

which he played all nine innings, was "spotty." During the 2003 off-season, Damon suffered from extremely painful headaches, which he said came every afternoon around two o'clock. His headaches began to diminish after he started to see a chiropractor in the off-season.

In *Idiot,* Damon says that the migraines were so bad that he didn't shave when he was having them—thus giving birth to the new, bushy-bearded, heavily maned "caveman" persona that he sported throughout 2004. "When I shave, I'm thorough," he wrote. "I spend a lot of time, and I just didn't feel like spending 30 or so minutes shaving. So that was another reason for my full beard when I arrived at camp."

Even with Damon's health in doubt, Game 5 against the A's began to rip apart the seams of the Curse of the Bambino. Manny Ramírez's key three-run bomb and Damon's survival of the scary, head-on-head collision with infielder Jackson were only subplots. The big news was that, finally, the Sox held on in a clutch game and, all of a sudden for Damon and his band of Cowboys, it was "New York here we come."

8

Redemption

Johnny Damon had played football in high school and had engaged in some violent collisions on the gridiron—but nothing like his tumble with teammate Damian Jackson that night in Oakland. Damon suffered a major concussion—he said later that he had not been hit that hard since Warren Sapp, a future NFL Pro Bowler, knocked him out during a high school football game.

Suddenly, Red Sox manager Grady Little found himself in a bind. He knew that having Damon in his lineup would greatly enhance the Red Sox's chances of upending the hated Yankees and moving on to the World Series. With Damon battling a concussion, though, he was in no position to play.

After traveling back to New York for the first game of the championship series, Damon approached Little and said he

Johnny Damon, still groggy from the concussion he suffered two days before, sat in the dugout during the opener of the 2003 American League Championship Series against the Yankees. He did not play in the first two games of the series and has said he can only vaguely remember what happened in those games.

was available to pinch-hit. The manager took one look at the banged-up Damon, now sporting a black eye the size of a small cantaloupe, and gently waved him off. "You don't look like you're all there, son," Little said. "You don't even sound right."

During the first two games of the series, with the Red Sox winning the first behind knuckleball wizard Tim Wakefield and the Bombers winning the second behind the crafty Andy Pettitte, Damon would try to get ready if he was needed, swinging a bat in the clubhouse and stretching in case he had to play in the field. Every time Damon thought he would be needed, however, Little brushed him off with a calm but stern "sit down, boy."

Finally, before Game 3, with Yankee ace—and former Red Sox hurler—Roger Clemens toeing the hill for New York, Little called Damon's name, penciling him in as the leadoff hitter and center fielder. Later, Damon would not recall much about the game, but he did manage three hits off Clemens.

Damon's predicament in Game 3 was overshadowed by a bench-clearing brawl triggered by a Pedro Martínez fastball that hit Yankee Karim Garcia. Damon had been around the Red Sox long enough to know that the ill temper between the two teams was genuine, not manufactured like some other rivalries he had seen. Damon ran in from center field and, still dazed from his injury, hung back with Yankee first baseman and old Oakland A's teammate Jason Giambi, who acted as a bodyguard for Damon and kept some of the rougher action away from him. Out of the corner of his eye, Damon noticed Yankee coach Don Zimmer being knocked to the ground by Martínez. All bedlam broke loose at that point, and it was all the umpires could do to keep both teams from baseball's version of a rugby scrum.

The Yankees had the last laugh, winning Game 3, but the Red Sox roared back behind the masterful Wakefield in Game 4. With Yankee lefty David Wells throwing sharp curveballs all day, the BoSox's bats went silent and New York took Game 5.

Damon's close friend John Burkett would get the call for the Red Sox in Game 6. Burkett was one of those clubhouse leaders that winning teams had to have to capture championships. An avowed football fan, Burkett started a clubhouse football pool that united the Red Sox as a team, as the players argued over the Patriots and the Colts. The pool generally kept everyone loose in the otherwise pressure-packed atmosphere that always defined a Red Sox-Yankees play-off series.

With the game tied in the seventh inning, a weakened Damon worked Yankee reliever Félix Heredia for a key bases-loaded walk, which turned out to be the winning run in a 9-6 Red Sox victory. With the series tied after six games, both teams would regroup the next night in Yankee Stadium for the deciding Game 7 and a chance to move on to the World Series—and, for the Red Sox, a chance to finally exorcise some long-held curses and demons.

GAME 7

It was a dream pitching matchup—Roger Clemens versus Pedro Martínez—and the Red Sox got the best of the Yankees early. Home runs by Trot Nixon and Kevin "Cowboy Up" Millar gave the Sox a 5-2 lead going into the bottom of the eighth inning. Damon and the Sox looked like a shoo-in for a victory and a date with the Florida Marlins, who had ousted the tough-luck Chicago Cubs in the National League Championship Series.

But, as always with the Red Sox, good fortune took a holiday, and the Yankees scored three times in the inning to tie the game. Damon felt helpless as the Yankees teed off on the now-tired Pedro Martínez. Worse, the Yankees brought in their All-Star relief pitcher Mariano Rivera, and the future Hall of Famer shut the Sox down for three straight innings. In the bottom of the eleventh inning, Yankee third baseman Aaron Boone broke the hearts of Red Sox fans all over New England with a long home run to left off of Wakefield—a knuckleball that didn't knuckle, Wakefield would say after the game.

In a somber Red Sox locker room after the game, Damon slowly took off his uniform, taking time to walk over and console the crestfallen Wakefield. Damon felt that he had not played well, that the head injury had slowed his game down and kept his usually reliable bat from erupting for some key hits during the series.

He knew that he had had a good year—166 hits, 32 doubles, 12 home runs, 6 triples, 103 runs scored, and a .273 average from the leadoff position. He had also had 10 hits in the postseason—four after the injury—and Damon had patrolled center field with his usually style and panache.

But it wasn't enough. Losing to the Yankees had seen to that. Next year would be different.

A DREAM SEASON BEGINS

The 2004 season started and ended with a bang for Damon and the Red Sox. Individually, it would be one of his best seasons ever.

That year, he was second in the league in runs scored with 123. Damon also batted .304 with 20 home runs and 94 RBIs, and showed improved patience at the plate. His RBI total was fairly amazing for a leadoff hitter—in fact, Damon was only the fourth leadoff batter in the history of Major League Baseball to drive in more than 90 runs in a season.

The Red Sox were refortified and rejuvenated in 2004. Only five outs away from the World Series the year before, Damon and his teammates liked their chances, especially with the addition in the off-season of All-Star pitcher Curt Schilling from Arizona and ace reliever Keith Foulke from Oakland. The Red Sox had fired Grady Little after the 2003 championship-series loss, so a new manager was in town, too. Terry Francona, the former manager of the Philadelphia Phillies, whose surly fans basically rode him out of town, seemed like the perfect fit for a jelling team that was so close to winning a pennant.

To loosen up the atmosphere, some of the players joined ringleaders Johnny Damon and Kevin Millar in buying new motorcycles, which they rode up and down the streets of Fort Myers, Florida, at night during spring training. Back home in Boston, Pedro Martínez sprung for a massage chair in the Sox's

With his leaping catch, Johnny Damon robbed the Orioles' David Segui of a home run during a game on April 7, 2004, at Camden Yards in Baltimore. The magic of the 2004 season was beginning early for Damon and the Red Sox.

locker room, away from the prying eyes of the media. Damon and his mates loved the chair, which faced a new Sony TV and DVD player. The Sox were a loose bunch.

With a one-two pitching punch of Martínez and Schilling, the Red Sox broke out of the gate fast. Damon had a five-hit game during the season's first series against the Orioles. He also made a great leaping catch to rob Baltimore's David Segui of a home run. Soon the Yankees, along with marquee free agent Alex Rodriguez, came to town, but the Sox were ready, taking three of four games against the Bombers. A week later in New York, the Sox swept the Yankees in three games. Damon was a huge contributor, racing to grab a shot to the gap by Yankee power hitter Gary Sheffield to save one game.

By the All-Star break, Damon was having a great year, batting .321, and the Red Sox were a nose ahead of the Oakland A's in the wild-card race.

FIGHTING THE YANKEES

Right away, after the All-Star Game, the Red Sox would go at it with the Yankees. On July 24, an ugly brawl erupted after the Yankees' Rodriguez was brushed back by Boston pitcher Bronson Arroyo. Rodriguez had some harsh words for Arroyo, harsh enough that Sox catcher Jason Varitek stepped in and shoved Rodriguez in the face with his catcher's mitt. Bedlam ensued, with players racing in and trading punches as both benches emptied.

To Damon, the frenetic scene was welcome—it showed that the Red Sox were sticking together and solidifying as a team. The Red Sox had been trailing in the nationally televised game but came back on the strength of a Bill Mueller home run to beat the Yankees. The Red Sox used that game as a springboard to make a big run.

The next day, Damon hit a three-run homer off the Yankees' José Contreras, cementing another victory. A few days later, on July 31, the Red Sox traded popular shortstop

Nomar Garciaparra, bringing in some much-needed defense but giving up Garciaparra's lively bat.

The Sox kept the heat on the Yankees, winning series against the Angels, the A's, and the Devil Rays. Damon and

★ ☆ ☆ ☆ ☆ ☆

DAMON'S CHARITY

There's an obvious fun-loving side to Johnny Damon. He likes to play pranks and engage in plenty of high jinks—inside and outside of the locker room. Damon, though, also has a giving, more serious side—as seen through the Johnny Damon Foundation, which raises and donates funds to charitable groups.

Damon has also been actively involved with the Wounded Warrior Project, serving as a national spokesman for the program. The Wounded Warrior Project assists the men and women of the U.S. military who have suffered grave injuries during the war on terrorism. Services provided by the project include benefits counseling, rehabilitation, adaptive sports opportunities, and advocacy programs.

"I have deep gratitude for the men and women who have been severely wounded while fighting for our freedoms and way of life," Damon said. "My goal is to ensure their challenges and sacrifices are recognized."

Besides the Wounded Warrior Project, Damon's foundation also has relationships with Memorial Sloan-Kettering Cancer Center in New York City and the Edgewood Children's Ranch and Winnie Palmer Children's Hospital, both in Orlando.

Millar kept the team loose, by holding impromptu hockey games in the clubhouse and by playing constant pranks.

One day, before a game against the Yankees, a local reporter walked up to Damon and asked him how the team would handle the Yankees. "I don't know," Damon answered. "We're not going to try and figure that out. We're just a bunch of idiots."

A new moniker was born, with both the fans and the press catching on. The Red Sox were indeed a band of idiots, and the biggest and proudest idiot of all was Johnny Damon. The Red Sox were having fun and winning games, making the play-offs as the wild-card team after finishing with a 98–64 record. After easily disposing of the Anaheim Angels in the American League Division Series, three games to none, they were ready to exact some revenge on the Yankees.

STILL MORE YANKEE BATTLES

It was another Hunt for Red Sox October, as the signs around Fenway would state—this time, the Red Sox were ready, although it did not seem that way at first.

Game 1 was in Yankee Stadium, with the Yankees jumping out to a quick lead. Soon, the Sox were down 8-0 and that old sinking feeling was starting to creep in across Red Sox Nation.

The Red Sox, though, came back and made a game of it. They scored five runs in the seventh inning, and with a two-run triple from David Ortiz, Boston closed the lead to one run. But Yankee relief ace Mariano Rivera was able to shut the door and close out the Sox, 10-7. Damon had not played well, striking out four times, but he was glad to see that nobody had their head down in the locker room. Nobody was giving an inch.

"We can beat these guys," Damon said to himself. "No doubt about it."

The great Pedro Martínez was pitching for the Sox in Game 2. Martínez had caused a fuss earlier in the year when he admitted after a tough loss that the Yankees were "his Daddy." What he meant was that the Yankees seemed to have the upper hand in the games he pitched, and the prideful Martínez was clearly frustrated when he said it.

Still, the Yankee fans and the baseball writers jumped all over the comment. Plastered on the pages of the New York tabloids on the morning of Game 2 were headlines like "Who's Your Daddy?" Clearly, Martínez had struck a nerve.

That did not stop him from pitching well. The problem was that Yankee starter Jon Lieber, a tall, lanky sinker-ball pitcher in the style of the Red Sox's own Derek Lowe, pitched even better.

Damon tried to do his part, working Lieber for a 16-pitch at-bat in the sixth inning before lining out. The Sox, though, came up short again, losing 3-1 to the Yankees.

Rain forced a delay before Game 3 back in Boston, but the weather did not take away the momentum from the streaking Yankees. They exploded with 19 runs on a wet Saturday night in Boston, and it looked as if Halloween had come early in Beantown. Final score: 19-8, Yankees on top.

ON THE COMEBACK TRAIL

After the game, the Red Sox regrouped in the locker room. Far from dejected, players like Damon and Curt Schilling said nothing was impossible, although coming back from a three-game deficit against the Yankees sure seemed to be. In fact, in all of baseball history, no team had ever come all the way back from a three-game deficit. To do so against the Yankees would be making history. The Yanks were cocky—perhaps too cocky. Gary Sheffield told the New York press that the Sox were "walking disasters." Other Yankees said the Red Sox were finished.

Those comments by the Yankees fueled the Red Sox. And just before Game 4, Damon spoke to his teammates in the clubhouse. According to *Idiot*, Damon said:

> This could be the last game a bunch of us play together. Let's not make it our last. Let's put it all together. We're not supposed to win. I haven't hit. I've let us down so far, but guess what, I'm going to keep going strong. We need everybody to pitch in. There's no pressure on us. All the pressure's on them. Let's not make this our last game together. Let's serve our Red Sox Nation proud. If we go out, we go out with a fight.

A home run by Alex Rodriguez gave the Yankees a quick lead, but the Sox fought back with a single by Big Papi—David Ortiz—that scored Damon and Orlando Cabrera. By the ninth inning, the Yankees were clinging to a 4-3 lead and it looked like lights out for the Sox with Mariano Rivera on the mound. Kevin Millar walked, and Dave Roberts, pinch-running for Millar, stole second base. He scored one batter later on a clutch single by Bill Mueller. Suddenly, the Red Sox had life. To Damon, it seemed that the Yankees were sagging a little. Then, in the bottom of the twelfth inning, Big Papi did it again— hitting a long home run to clinch the victory for the Red Sox.

Game 5 was another barn-burner, with Ortiz coming up big once again with a game-winning single in the fourteenth inning; Damon scored the winning run after working Yankee reliever Esteban Loaiza for a walk. Damon had only two hits in 24 at-bats so far during the series, so Damon was happy to contribute with the run.

The players on both teams were exhausted, but at least the Red Sox had life. Going back to New York and winning two games was more than possible.

Johnny Damon celebrated with his teammates after hitting his second-inning grand slam in the final game of the 2004 American League Championship Series against the Yankees. The Curse was in its last gasps.

Game 6 found the hobbled Curt Schilling on the hill, pitching heroically. He had injured his ankle in the division series against Anaheim, and the injury had affected his pitching in Game 1 of the championship series. Hours before Game 6, Schilling had surgery on his ankle to allow him to pitch. The Sox scratched out a run and then another three runs on a big home run by Mark Bellhorn. It was as if a light switch went out in Yankee Stadium, draining the cavernous ballpark of any energy.

All of a sudden, the Yankees were the ones on the ropes—and Damon and his teammates knew it. With Derek Lowe starting Game 7 and pitching as if his life depended on it, Johnny Damon took over from there.

A grand slam by Damon off Javier Vázquez in the second inning caused a din in Boston that could be heard in the Bronx. Now, the Sox were up 6-0 and the Yankees were gasping for air. The Red Sox and Damon, though, stepped on their neck, instead.

In the fourth inning, with Orlando Cabrera on first after an eight-pitch walk, Damon walloped another home run, this one into Yankee Stadium's upper deck in right field. Another home run, a solo shot by Bellhorn in the eighth inning, iced it for the Red Sox. A stunned Yankee Stadium crowd sat in disbelief. The Red Sox had done it—coming all the way back from a three-games-to-none deficit to beat the Yankees. From there, the Red Sox went on to the World Series.

For Johnny Damon and the Red Sox, and for their army of fans in Red Sox Nation, the Curse of the Bambino was about to be obliterated. The Yankees were toast, and Damon and the Red Sox were the toast of the baseball world.

Idiots, indeed.

9

After the Curse

Although the Red Sox were well-stocked with great pitchers like Pedro Martínez and Curt Schilling—both future Hall of Famers—it was the big bats that the Sox carried that made most of the news.

In fact, the Red Sox, in the previous season, had a better slugging percentage—meaning that they hit more doubles, triples, and home runs—than the 1927 Yankees, the greatest-hitting team of all time. That team, whose lineup was known as "Murderers Row," had Babe Ruth, Lou Gehrig, Tony Lazzeri, and a host of other mashers.

The fact that the Red Sox could still bring that type of firepower into the 2004 World Series spelled trouble for the St. Louis Cardinals, the National League champions, who had a packed lineup of their own with Scott Rolen, Albert Pujols, Larry Walker, and Edgar Rentería.

The Red Sox, however, set the tone early in Game 1 with 11 runs in a victory. Damon led the game off with a double on a 3-2 pitch and subsequently scored on a David Ortiz home run.

The Sox followed that up with a 6-2 win, with Curt Schilling and Jason Varitek leading the way. Pedro Martínez kept the pressure on in Game 3 with a masterpiece, shutting down the Cards 4-1 behind a Manny Ramírez home run.

Damon felt that the Red Sox were confident going into Game 4—but not too confident. They had seen what had happened to the Yankees in the American League Championship Series. The Yanks had a three-game lead and they lost, didn't they? Damon did not want his teammates to think negatively about that, but they could not be too confident, either.

Fortunately for the Red Sox, Damon would take matters into his own hands, slamming a screamer into the right-field seats for a leadoff home run in the first inning. That took the fight out of the Cards right away and, thanks to a great pitching performance by Derek Lowe and a clutch, bases-loaded double by Trot Nixon, the Red Sox, leading 3-0, entered the bottom of the ninth inning poised to make history.

The Cards would not go quietly. Pujols opened the inning with a single, and all of Red Sox Nation gripped their chairs in suspense. The Sox couldn't possibly blow it again, could they? Not to worry. Red Sox relief specialist Keith Foulke shut down the next three Cardinal hitters, the last on an easy grounder back to Foulke, who calmly flipped the ball to first for the out. Game, series, and match to the Boston Red Sox, who had finally done it—they had beaten the Curse of the Bambino and were now the 2004 world champions.

In celebration, Damon and his teammates formed a mosh pit near the pitcher's mound. Players leaped on one another,

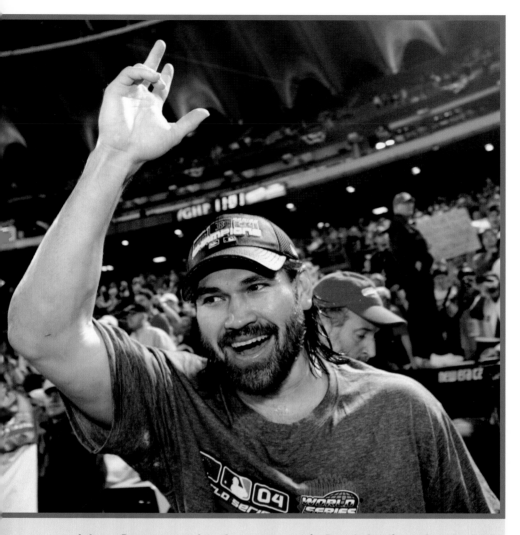

Johnny Damon waved to the spectators in Busch Stadium after the Red Sox beat the Cardinals in Game 4 to sweep the 2004 World Series. In that game, Damon hit a leadoff home run, dealing a blow to the Cardinals right from the start.

hugging and pounding each other on the back. A Hollywood movie about the Red Sox, called *Fever Pitch* and starring Jimmy Fallon and Drew Barrymore, filmed its climactic scene right there in the middle of the scrum, with the two co-stars kissing to celebrate the victory on the field. It was a Hollywood ending all right—for Damon, for his teammates, and for Red Sox fans everywhere.

Damon took advantage of the hoopla, appearing on *Saturday Night Live* the following Saturday and on *Late Night with David Letterman* on Monday. He had a scene or two in *Fever Pitch*, and there was even talk of a reality TV show.

The chaos increased with Damon's marriage to his long-time girlfriend, Michelle Mangan—an extravagant affair in

★ ★ ★ ★ ★ ★

A CLOSE SHAVE

Johnny Damon proved to be a big hit with women in Boston. His good looks, easy-going charisma, and long, flowing, jet-black hair and bushy beard made him a heartthrob in Red Sox Nation.

Plenty of fans thought that Damon looked like Jesus Christ, and signs around town sprouted up, asking, "What Would Johnny Damon Do?"—a takeoff on the phrase, "What Would Jesus Do?"

Damon, though, did not let his hair and beard grow on purpose. After his terrible head-on collision with a teammate in the 2003 play-offs, Damon began to suffer headaches—to the point where it hurt to shave or have his hair cut. So, to alleviate the pain, he stopped shaving and let his hair grow.

But Damon was good-natured about it. Late in 2004, he helped raise funds for the Boston Public Library system by having his beard shaved in front of hundreds of fans. He commented that libraries had helped him during his youth.

Damon joked to the fans that nobody needed to worry—he could grow a full beard back in two weeks. Which is exactly what he did.

December that saw all of Damon's family and friends joining together for the wedding. Now, Damon was in a great place—happily married, a World Series hero, and a member of the first Red Sox championship team in more than 80 years.

Little did he know that change—big change—was on the way.

THE DISMANTLING OF THE IDIOTS

Almost immediately, the 2004 Red Sox team—the "idiots," as Damon had called them—was coming apart. Pedro Martínez, Derek Lowe, and shortstop Orlando Cabrera moved on to other teams. The Sox would release Mark Bellhorn during the 2005 season. Damon knew that the reality of baseball was that money ruled—the Sox could not possibly keep everyone from the championship team, so they tried to keep everyone they could, then add new players into the mix as needed. Coincidentally, one of the first big free-agent signings by the Red Sox was Edgar Rentería—the St. Louis Cardinal shortstop who had made the last out of the 2004 World Series.

Damon felt secure, though. He knew that the Red Sox thought the world of him and that he would be rewarded with a new contract soon. He had one more year on his contract with the Red Sox, but 2005 proved to be something of a disappointment. Damon got hurt, banging his shoulder into the outfield wall while making a play in May. He was also hit by a pitch on the wrist in August and jammed his shoulder making a catch in September. Despite not being able to play at full strength, Damon batted .316, best among the Red Sox. He scored 117 runs, hit 10 home runs, had 75 RBIs, and stole 18 bases.

The magic of the 2004 season did not carry over into 2005 for the Red Sox. They were leading the American League East by four games in early September but blew that lead and ended up tied with the Yankees at the end of the season. The Yankees were awarded the division title because they had won

During the 2005 season, Johnny Damon suffered several injuries—including banging his shoulder here when he crashed into the outfield wall in a May 31 game against the Orioles. His teammate Trot Nixon is seen chasing down Jay Gibbons's triple.

the season series against the Red Sox. Boston, though, made the play-offs as the wild-card team, then lost in the American League Division Series to the Chicago White Sox, three games to none.

THE YANKEES COME CALLING

Soon after the 2005 season, the Red Sox made noises about offering Damon a big contract—but something told Damon that, after all his hard work and success in Boston, he deserved more. Damon's agent, Scott Boras, had set a seven-year, $84 million deal as the target price for Damon. The Sox, though, offered a four-year, $40 million proposal. Then, in early December, the New York Yankees contacted Damon.

Would he come play in the Bronx for $52 million?

Damon struggled with the decision. On the one hand, the Red Sox had been loyal, the fans were great, and they all had enjoyed the ride of a lifetime in winning the World Series in 2004—and handing the Yankees their worst play-off loss ever in the process. What could top that?

On the other hand, Damon would make enough cash that he and his family would never have to worry about money again. That meant a lot to a kid from Orlando who had to work for every penny growing up. Plus, there was no bigger stage than Yankee Stadium. A crowd favorite like Damon could get a lot of mileage from wearing the most visible and historic uniform in all of sports—the classic pinstripes of the New York Yankees.

It was a tough decision. Leaving the Red Sox for the Yankees was the equivalent of Luke Skywalker leaving the Jedi to go over to the Dark Side.

A few years back, two Red Sox greats—Roger Clemens and Wade Boggs—had signed with the Yankees, and both had won championships. But their return trips to formerly friendly Fenway were nightmares: Boos cascaded down from the cheap seats, and their own families did not feel safe sitting in the stands. Red Sox Nation would not let their former heroes off the hook—they made them pay a stiff price for wearing the hated pinstripes.

In the end, the Yankees showed Damon that they wanted him more than the Red Sox did. The Bombers needed to replace their aging superstar center fielder Bernie Williams. With Damon in a star-studded lineup along with Derek Jeter, Alex Rodriguez, Jason Giambi, and Gary Sheffield, no baseball would be safe. Damon, as one of the premier leadoff batters in the game, would be a valuable addition to such a lineup.

The Yankees knew that they were getting more than just a fleet-footed run-scoring machine. Damon was a great teammate in Boston, too. His fellow players loved him just as much as the fans did, and the Yankees—who were talented on the field but cold and unaccommodating off of it—needed a spark plug in the clubhouse as well as between the lines every night.

"People say Johnny was a leader on the Red Sox," said one Red Sox follower. "That's a mistake. Johnny was a consensus builder. He'd move from the Latinos to the blacks to the whites, just making sure everyone got along."

Even the Yankee players knew that. Rodriguez, whom Damon had publicly berated for an unsportsmanlike play in the 2004 championship series, picked up the phone that December and made his pitch for Damon to come to the Yankees.

Damon appreciated the gesture. "Alex mentioned that me, him, and Derek were all approaching a lot of milestones and how great it would be to reach them as teammates, but people could look back on us and forget the numbers and remember what we did together," Damon told one reporter. "It meant a lot to me."

His bushy beard and long hair newly shorn, Johnny Damon tried on his Yankees jersey during a news conference announcing his signing with the team. Also attending were manager Joe Torre *(left)* and general manager Brian Cashman. Damon signed a four-year, $52 million contract with the Yankees in December 2005.

DECISION TIME

With their $52 million offer, "the Yankees just want me more," Damon thought. In one final 24-hour period, swayed by phone calls from Rodriguez and Red Sox teammates Kevin Millar and Bill Mueller, who told Damon to take care of his family first, he bucked the conventional odds and signed with the Yankees.

Johnny Damon, famed Yankee-slayer, was now a Bronx Bomber. As one press report put it, Red Sox Nation did not take the news well. Stephen Rodrick wrote in an article for *New York* magazine:

> On December 20, Damon agreed to a deal with the Yankees. All of New England was apoplectic. The Red Sox had let their beloved team leader go. The Yankees—the freakin' Yankees!—had signed him. Soon came the pictures of Damon wearing a Yankees jersey and lopping off his mane at the Boss's request. Back in Boston, Damon's jersey was being sold at a steep discount, with DEMON replacing DAMON on the back.

It was not how Damon wanted it to end in Boston, his favorite place to play baseball in the world. He felt mixed emotions about the deal but was hopeful that the fans would, in time, understand. He just wanted another challenge, another hill to climb. It was time to take another challenge and move on.

That, after all, is how Damon lived his life. When one goal was accomplished, he crossed it off of his list and moved on. Now that he had helped destroy the Curse of the Bambino, he would put all of his energy into playing in Yankee Stadium—The House That Ruth Built, as they say in New York.

In the Pinstripes

If people thought that the bright lights of New York City and the heavy history of the black pinstripes were going to change happy-go-lucky Johnny Damon, the Yankees' new center fielder seemed intent on proving them wrong in 2006.

Yankee fans were glad to have him aboard, as were his new teammates, who took to Damon's jovial nature quickly. Even without his beard and long hair, Damon was recognized as a different sort of player than New York fans were used to. For one, he was not afraid to speak his mind, even if that was not always the most diplomatic move to make.

When his former team got off to a hot start in 2006 while the Yankees lagged behind, Damon was not going to sugar-coat the situation. He told reporters that New York's bad injury bug was all that was keeping the vaunted Yankee squad from overtaking Boston. He continued to support Yankee hitters who were battling injuries, battling slumps—if he was a Yankee, Damon was behind him.

Of course, Damon's quick embrace of the ways of the "Evil Empire" did not sit well with his former fans back in Boston. Despite their team's success, Sox fans had not gotten over the center fielder's defection. They still talked about it on the radio, on TV, and in the bars. The fact that Damon's replacement in Boston, former Indian Coco Crisp, was not living up to expectations did not help matters.

☆ ☆ ☆ ☆ ☆

FAN-FRIENDLY

Johnny Damon is always quick to note that he would be nowhere without the support of baseball fans. He knows that the folks who stop him around town or ask him for autographs at the ballpark are great baseball fans and he tries to accommodate as many of them as possible. Even after a brutal loss, the fans and the media know they can count on Damon for a quick interview or an autograph.

In his first training camp with the Yankees in Florida in 2006, Damon proved how humble he could be. As the Yankee players left the field, hundreds of fans began to shout out their names. Only one Yankee stopped—the new one, Johnny Damon. He signed a few balls and programs and then apologized to the fans for not being able to sign some more—he had to get his running in.

Always the court jester, Damon joked to the crowd that he would much rather sign autographs than run but his manager might be upset that he was not getting into shape for the season.

The fans at Fenway cheered—not for Johnny Damon but for his result, after he flied out during the first inning of a game on May 1, 2006. The game was Damon's first one back in Boston as a New York Yankee. The Red Sox fans booed him whenever he came to bat and threw fake money at him.

BACK AT FENWAY

But Damon would be sorely mistaken if he was expecting a warm welcome and pleading calls for his return upon his first visit to Fenway Park as a Yankee on May 1, 2006. Each time he trotted to the plate, boos rained upon him from the Fenway grandstands. Fans mockingly chanted "John-ny, John-ny" and threw fake money at him.

When he tipped his cap to the crowd as a friendly gesture at one point during the game, Damon roused a few cheers, but there was no misinterpreting Boston's overall attitude: All was not forgiven. Coincidentally, Damon finished the game 0-for-4 at the plate, and the Yankees lost, 7-3.

Damon did not hold the fans' bitterness against Boston— he continued to tell newspapers that he would always love the city. He also kept on good terms with his former teammates, at one point hugging Boston slugger David Ortiz before the May 1 game.

There was no doubt, however, that Damon was a committed Yankee. When teammates around him started to fall to injuries, Damon held the fort, playing through pulls and pains to put together a fine first half of the season. He even played with a crack in one of the bones in his right foot. He did not make the All-Star team that July, but his worth to the ailing Yankees was more than mere statistics could tell.

By mid-summer, Damon and the Yanks were finally hitting their stride. Stars like Derek Jeter were performing well at the plate. More surprising, the Yankees also had a new ace on the mound, the previously unheard-of Chien-Ming Wang, who was picking up the slack of some of the struggling veterans on the pitching staff. Despite his injuries, Damon might have been the most productive Yankee of all, and his name came up in MVP talks as the season progressed.

By the middle of August, the Yankees had reclaimed the lead in the American League East and, to prove their dominance of the now injury-plagued Red Sox, swept their

East Coast rival in a pivotal five-game series at Fenway. As usual, New York was in the driver's seat as the play-offs approached.

Like Red Sox fans, Yankee fans were a fickle bunch, however. Merely getting to the postseason was not good enough. Year in and year out, club owner George Steinbrenner spent more money than anyone else in Major League Baseball to get the Yankees to the World Series, and New York expected a title. As far as Yankee fans were concerned, Damon wasn't worth a dime until he delivered in October.

Unfortunately for him, that delivery would stop short of arrival in 2006. As powerful as the Yankees lineup was that year, the team had the misfortune of running into the eventual American League champs, the Detroit Tigers, in the division series. Damon and his fellow Yankee hitters were no match for Detroit's heralded young pitching staff, which overwhelmed New York with speed and precision. The Yankees lost in four games. Once again, the Yankees went into the off-season still searching for that elusive twenty-seventh championship.

Damon, however, at least had proved himself worthy to the Yankee fan base on some level. Not only had he contributed to an often sickly lineup despite his own injuries, but Damon also finished with respectable numbers: a .285 batting average, 80 RBIs, 25 stolen bases, and a career-best 24 homers.

PROMISE IN 2007

Heading into the 2007 season, the Yankees were once again looking like a team to be reckoned with. New York had jettisoned some of the team's underachieving veterans, most notably ace left-hander Randy Johnson, and made several subtle deals to solidify a team that had won the American League East in 2006 by 10 games.

And once again, Damon figured to be an important leader on a stocked Yankee roster. But the injuries from his 2006 campaign lingered into 2007, hampering Damon throughout much of the spring. In fact, the trouble began on Opening Day, when Damon was sidelined with a calf injury.

Damon was not the only Yankee suffering through a tough 2007, however. Aside from third baseman Alex Rodriguez, who was enjoying a spectacular start, New York was abysmal for most of the first half. The team's prize off-season signing, former Japanese league pitcher Kei Igawa, had imploded before the season had barely begun. The rest of the pitching staff could not get past the fourth or fifth inning before manager Joe Torre would have to go to the bullpen for relief. Meanwhile, the resurgent Red Sox were the hottest team in baseball.

Once again, the dire situation did not bother Damon too much, or at least he did not let it show. He was off to one of his worst starts ever at the plate, hitting around .250 by June, but he shrugged off the injuries as if they were a temporary inconvenience. He had a tougher time convincing the Yankee faithful, however, who were expecting to see the indestructible Damon of old, the one who rarely ever missed a start. Fans began to question his signing.

As usual, however, Damon was helping the team in any way he could. When Jason Giambi went out with an injury in the spring, Damon filled his role as the designated hitter. Melky Cabrera took Damon's spot in center field. As the season progressed, Cabrera cemented his place in center field, and Damon was used part time as a designated hitter and outfielder. Damon was never comfortable with the prospect of being a part-time player on the Yankees, but he refused to give in to defeat.

Eventually, the season began to come around for Damon and the Yankees. The team caught fire in August and began to pick away at Boston's lead in the American League East,

Giving the Yankees the lead, Johnny Damon crossed home plate after hitting a two-run home run against Boston on August 28, 2007. His homer gave New York a 5-3 victory, the first of three in a crucial series against the Red Sox.

which had been 14 games at one point. By the end of August, New York was entering a pivotal series with the Red Sox that would reveal if the Yankees had enough left to take the division away.

In the opener in New York, a tightly contested game entered the bottom of the seventh inning tied at 3-3. After the leadoff hitter got on, Damon strode to the plate to face Boston's Daisuke Matsuzaka. As if to signal that the nagging injuries of recent months were a thing of the past, Damon crushed the first pitch over the right-field fence. As he leaned to watch the ball sail into the stands, Damon did a quick hop and started his trot around the bases. Yankee fans showered their star with cheers, and Damon responded in turn by waving to the crowd from the dugout afterward.

The Yankees went on to sweep the Sox in the three-game series and get within five games of their rival in the standings. In September, that lead dipped all the way to a game and a half. Later that month, the Yankees clinched a play-off spot, this time as arguably one of the hottest teams in baseball.

Damon, of course, was credited by Torre for being a major catalyst in the Yankees' turnaround. He was known to scream and shout in the dugout, inspiring his teammates as much with his words as his play.

Even as a creaky veteran, Damon played the game with the exuberance he had as a prodigy in Orlando. And, as the Red Sox found out, neither injuries nor an insurmountable division lead could keep their former center fielder from willing himself to victory.

Unfortunately, as much as he tried, he could not will the Yankees to victory in the postseason. New York faced the Cleveland Indians in the American League Division Series and lost the first two games in Cleveland. Damon gave the team and the Yankee fans hope in Game 3 when he hit a three-run homer in the fifth inning to give New York a 5-3 lead. The Yankees went on to win the game, 8-4. No such magic occurred in the fourth game, though, as Cleveland took the series with a 6-4 victory. It was now seven years since the Yankees' last World Series win.

After the season, Torre turned down the Yankees' one-year contract offer, which would have cut his pay, to return as manager. The Yankees hired Joe Girardi to replace Torre. Girardi, a former catcher with the Yankees, was named the National League Manager of the Year in 2006 when he was manager of the Florida Marlins.

Damon met with Girardi in November 2007 and was pleased with what Girardi told him. "He seems to be an awesome guy," Damon said, according to the *New York Times*. "I'm looking forward to playing for him. He just said, 'You're going to be my leadoff hitter and play left field.'"

Whether Johnny Damon can lead the Yankees back to their days of glory is unknown. What is clear is that Damon lives his life on his own terms and will stop at nothing to win, whether it was as a shy high school kid or as the diamond Messiah in baseball-mad Boston.

Whatever happens, Damon already has his place in baseball history. Not bad for a military brat from Orlando.

STATISTICS

JOHNNY DAMON
Primary position: Center field (Also LF)

Full name: Johnny David Damon • Born: November 5, 1973, Fort Riley, Kansas • Height: 6'2" • Weight: 205 lbs. • Teams: Kansas City Royals (1995–2000); Oakland Athletics (2001); Boston Red Sox (2002–2005); New York Yankees (2006–present)

YEAR	TEAM	G	AB	H	HR	RBI	BA
1995	KCR	47	188	53	3	23	.282
1996	KCR	145	517	140	6	50	.271
1997	KCR	146	472	130	8	48	.275
1998	KCR	161	642	178	18	66	.277
1999	KCR	145	583	179	14	77	.307
2000	KCR	159	655	214	16	88	.327
2001	OAK	155	644	165	9	49	.256
2002	BOS	154	623	178	14	63	.286
2003	BOS	145	608	166	12	67	.273
2004	BOS	150	621	189	20	94	.304
2005	BOS	148	624	197	10	75	.316
2006	NYY	149	593	169	24	80	.285
2007	NYY	141	533	144	12	63	.270
TOTAL		1,845	7,303	2,102	166	843	.288

Key: KCR = Kansas City Royals; OAK = Oakland Athletics; BOS = Boston Red Sox; NYY = New York Yankees; G = Games; AB = At-bats; H = Hits; HR = Home runs; RBI = Runs batted in; BA = Batting average

CHRONOLOGY

1973 **November 5** Born at Fort Riley, Kansas.

1992 Earns scholarship to the University of Florida.

Drafted by the Kansas City Royals as the thirty-fifth pick overall.

Plays for the Gulf Coast Royals and is named the Gulf Coast League's No. 1 prospect.

1993 Plays for Rockford Royals in the Class A Midwest League.

1994 Plays for the Wilmington Blue Rocks in the high-Class A Carolina League; the league's managers name him most exciting player.

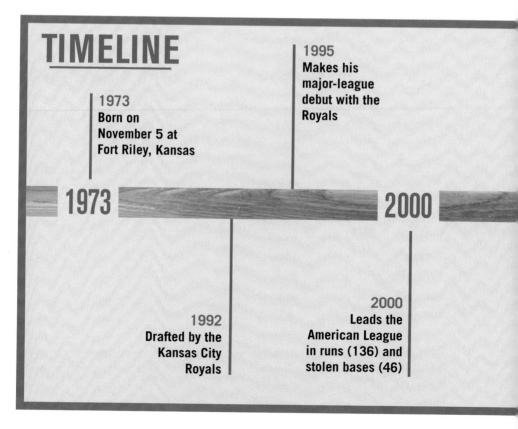

TIMELINE

1973
Born on November 5 at Fort Riley, Kansas

1995
Makes his major-league debut with the Royals

1973

2000

1992
Drafted by the Kansas City Royals

2000
Leads the American League in runs (136) and stolen bases (46)

1995   Begins the season playing for the Wichita Wranglers of the Class AA Texas League.

       August 12 Makes his major-league debut with the Kansas City Royals and goes 3-for-5.

1996   Hits .271 in his first full season with the Royals.

1999   Hits .307, the first season his batting average is over .300.

2000   Leads the American League in runs scored (136) and stolen bases (46); hits a career-best .327.

2001   Traded to the Oakland Athletics; plays in the postseason for the first time, though the A's lose to

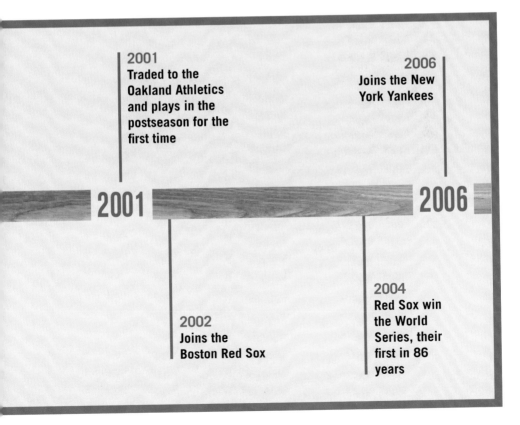

2001
Traded to the
Oakland Athletics
and plays in the
postseason for the
first time

2006
Joins the New
York Yankees

2001

2006

2002
Joins the
Boston Red Sox

2004
Red Sox win
the World
Series, their
first in 86
years

the New York Yankees in the American League Division Series.

December 21 Signs a four-year, $31 million contract with the Boston Red Sox.

2002   Hits .286 in his first season with the Red Sox and scores 118 runs; leads the club with 31 stolen bases.

2003   Suffers concussion in collision with Damian Jackson during the American League Division Series; Red Sox lose the American League Championship Series to the Yankees.

2004   Hits grand slam in Game 7 of the American League Championship Series to help the Red Sox defeat the Yankees; Red Sox become the first team in major-league history to win a seven-game series after trailing three games to none.

Red Sox sweep the St. Louis Cardinals to win the World Series, their first world championship since 1918.

2005   **December 20** Agrees to a four-year, $52 million deal with the New York Yankees.

2006   Hits .285 with a career-high 24 home runs in his first season with the Yankees.

GLOSSARY

assist   The official scorer awards an assist to every defensive player who fields or touches the ball (after it is hit by the batter) before a putout.

at-bat   An official turn at batting that is charged to a baseball player, except when the player walks, sacrifices, is hit by a pitched ball, or is interfered with by a catcher. At-bats are used to calculate a player's batting average and slugging percentage.

base on balls   The awarding of first base to a batter after a pitcher throws four balls. Also known as a walk, it is "intentional" when the four balls are thrown on purpose to avoid pitching to a batter.

batter's box   The area to the left and right of home plate in which the batter must be standing for fair play to take place.

batting average   The number of hits a batter gets divided by the number of times the player is at bat. For example, 3 hits in 10 at-bats would be a .300 batting average.

bullpen   The area where pitchers and catchers warm up. The bullpen is usually behind the outfield fences or off to the side along the left or right base line.

bunt   A ball hit softly so that it rolls to a particular spot in the infield. A bunt is usually hit by holding the bat loosely and letting the ball bounce off it rather than swinging the bat.

changeup   A slow pitch thrown with the same motion as a fastball in order to deceive the batter.

curveball   A pitch that curves on its way to the plate, thanks to the spin a pitcher places on the ball when throwing. Also know as a "breaking ball."

cutoff man   A fielder who "cuts off" a long throw to a target. Often, the shortstop or second baseman is the cutoff man for a long throw from the outfield to third base or home plate.

designated hitter   In the American League, a player who bats each time for the pitcher. There is no designated hitter in the National League. Baseball is the only professional sport in which different rules apply in different sections of the league. The lack of consistency about the designated hitter is an ongoing debate.

disabled list   In Major League Baseball, the disabled list is a way for teams to remove injured players from their rosters. Other players can be called up as replacements during this time.

draft   Major League Baseball's mechanism for assigning amateur players to its teams. The draft order is determined based on the previous season's standings, with the team with the worst record receiving the first pick.

error   When a defensive player makes a mistake that results in a runner reaching base or advancing a base, an error is designated by the game's scorer.

farm team   A team that provides training and experience for young players, with the expectation that successful players will move to the major leagues.

fastball   A pitch that is thrown so that is has maximum speed. It can be gripped in any number of ways, most commonly touching two baseball seams (a two-seamer) with the index finger and middle finger, or across four seams (four-seamer).

five-tool player   A player who has excellent fielding skills, a good throwing arm, and the ability to steal bases and hit for both batting average and power.

free agent   A professional athlete who is free to negotiate a contract with any team.

full count   If a batter has three balls and two strikes, he or she has a full count.

games behind   A statistic used in team standings. It is figured by adding the difference in wins between a trailing team and the leader to the difference in losses, and dividing by two. So a team that is three games behind may trail by three in the win column and three in the loss column, or four and two, or any other combination of wins and losses totaling six.

grand slam   A home run with three runners on base, resulting in four runs for the offensive team. The grand slam is one of the most dramatic plays in baseball.

home run   When a batter hits a ball into the stands in fair territory, it is a home run. The batter may also hit an inside-the-park home run if the ball never leaves the playing field and the runner is able to reach home plate without stopping before being tagged by a defensive player. A home run counts as one run, and if there are any runners on base when a home run is hit, they too score.

knuckleball   A slow pitch that is thrown with little spin by gripping the ball with the knuckles or the tips of the fingers. The pitch moves erratically and unpredictably.

leadoff hitter   The first batter in the lineup. The job of the leadoff hitter is to get to first base any way he can—through a walk, a single, a bunt, even getting hit by a pitch—and then move into scoring position.

line drive   A batted ball, usually hit hard, that never gets too far off the ground. Typically a line drive will get beyond the infield without touching the ground, or will be hit directly at a player and be caught before it touches the ground.

lineup   A list that is presented to the umpire and opposing coach before the start of the game that contains the order in which the batters will bat as well as the defensive fielding positions they will play.

on-base percentage   The number of times a player reaches base divided by the number of plate appearances.

on deck   The offensive player in line to bat after the current batter is said to be on deck. Often the player on deck will swing a weighted bat to warm up and stay in an area called the on-deck circle.

pinch hitter   A player who substitutes for another teammate at bat.

pinch runner   A substitute base runner, often brought in during a critical situation. The pinch runner typically replaces a slower runner in the hope of stealing a base.

position player   A baseball player who plays any position other than pitcher.

run batted in (RBI)   A run batted in is generally given to a batter for each run scored as the result of his appearance at the plate.

rubber game   A term used for the fifth game of a five-game series or the seventh game of a seven-game series when the two teams have split the first four or six games, respectively.

sabermetrics   The study of baseball using nontraditional statistics. Traditional baseball-performance measurement focuses on batting average, hits, home runs, and earned run average. Sabermetrics tries to measure those statistics that predict winning and losing most accurately. On-base percentage and slugging percentage are two key sabermetric statistics.

short porch   When one of the outfield walls is closer to home plate than normal, the stadium is said to have a short porch.

sinker ball   A pitch, typically a fastball, that breaks sharply downward as it crosses the plate.

slugging percentage   The number of bases a player reaches divided by the number of at-bats. It is a measure of the power of a batter.

spring training   A period of practice and exhibition games in professional baseball that begins in late winter and goes until the start of the season in spring.

strike   A pitch that is swung at and missed or a pitch that is in the strike zone and is not swung at. A foul ball counts as a strike unless it would be the third strike. Three strikes and the batter is out.

strike zone   The area directly over home plate up to the batter's chest (roughly where the batter's uniform lettering is) and down to his or her knees. Different umpires have slightly different strike zones, and players only ask that they be consistent.

strike out looking   When a batter is called out on strikes without swinging at the third strike.

stolen base   When a runner successfully advances to the next base while the pitcher is delivering a pitch.

walk-off home run   A game-ending home run by the home team—so named because the losing team has to walk off the field.

World Series   The championship series of Major League Baseball. The Series is played between the pennant winners of the American League and the National League in a best-of-seven play-off.

BIBLIOGRAPHY

Damon, Johnny, with Peter Golenbock. *Idiot: Beating "The Curse" and Enjoying the Game of Life.* New York: Crown Publishers, 2005.

Hohler, Bob. "Johnny Damon, Superstar: Red Sox Outfielder Thrives in Spotlight." *Boston Globe.* July 11, 2005.

Johnson, Paul M. "Speed Damon." *Sport.* July 1996.

Massarotti, Tony, and John Harper. *A Tale of Two Cities: The 2004 Yankees-Red Sox Rivalry and the War for the Pennant.* Guilford, Conn.: The Lyons Press, 2005.

O'Nan, Stewart, and Stephen King. *Faithful: Two Diehard Boston Red Sox Fans Chronicle the Historic 2004 Season.* New York: Scribner, 2004.

Rafael, Dan, Mel Antonen, and Steve Wieberg. "Damon Headed to A's in Three-Team AL Trade." *USA Today.* January 9, 2001.

Rodrick, Stephen. "And an Idiot Shall Lead Them." *New York.* Available online at http://nymag.com/news/sports/16528/.

Shaughnessy, Dan. *Reversing the Curse.* Boston: Houghton Mifflin Co., 2005.

Silverman, Michael. "Johnny Be Good . . . and Fast." *Sporting News.* August 19, 2002.

Simmons, Bill. *Now I Can Die in Peace: How ESPN's Sports Guy Found Salvation with a Little Help from Nomar, Pedro, Shawshank, and the 2004 Red Sox.* Bristol, Conn.: ESPN, 2005.

Sorci, Rick. "Baseball Profile: Johnny Damon." *Baseball Digest.* July 2003.

Sussman, Matthew T. "Boston Might Not Like Johnny Damon Anymore." *Blogcritics Magazine.* May 2, 2006.

Available online at http://blogcritics.org/archives/2006/05/0
2/153040.php.

Topkin, Marc. "Idiot at Play." *St. Petersburg Times.*
April 22, 2005. Available online at http://www.sptimes.
com/2005/04/22/Sports/Idiot_at_play.shtml.

FURTHER READING

BOOKS

Christopher, Matt. *Great Moments in Baseball History.* New York: Little, Brown, 1996.

Golenbock, Peter. *Red Sox Nation: An Unexpurgated History of the Boston Red Sox.* Chicago: Triumph Books, 2005.

Lewis, Michael. *Moneyball: The Art of Winning an Unfair Game.* New York: W. W. Norton & Company, 2003.

MacKay, Claire. *Touching All the Bases: Baseball for Kids of All Ages.* Tonawanda, N.Y.: Firefly Books Ltd, 1996.

Mintzer, Rich. *The Everything Kids' Baseball Book.* Cincinnati: Adams Media Group, 2004.

Morgan, Joe. *Baseball for Dummies.* Hoboken, N.J.: Wiley Publishing, Inc., 2005.

Nowlin, Bill, and Jim Price. *Blood Feud: The Red Sox, the Yankees, and the Struggle of Good Versus Evil.* Burlington, Mass.: Rounder Books, 2005.

Stout, Glenn. *New York Yankees: Yesterday and Today.* Lincolnwood, Ill.: Publications International, 2007.

Stout, Glenn. *Yankees Century: 100 Years of New York Yankees Baseball.* Boston: Houghton Mifflin, 2002.

Vaccaro, Mike. *Emperors and Idiots: The Hundred-Year Rivalry Between the Yankees and the Red Sox, from the Very Beginning to the End of the Curse.* New York: Broadway Books, 2006.

Ward, Geoffrey C., and Ken Burns. *Baseball: An Illustrated History.* New York: Alfred A. Knopf, Inc., 1994.

WEB SITES

Baseball Almanac

http://www.baseball-almanac.com

Baseball Reference
http://www.baseball-reference.com

Johnny Damon Foundation
http://www.johnnydamonfoundation.org

The Johnny Damon Official Website
http://www.johnnydamon.net

The Official Site of the Boston Red Sox
http://boston.redsox.mlb.com

The Official Site of Major League Baseball
http://mlb.mlb.com

The Official Site of the New York Yankees
http://newyork.yankees.mlb.com

PICTURE CREDITS

INDEX

ABOUT THE AUTHOR

BRIAN O'CONNELL is a freelance writer based in Bucks County, Pennsylvania. A former Wall Street bond trader, O'Connell is the author of 15 books, including two best sellers. His work has also appeared in publications like *The Wall Street Journal, CBS Sportsline, NBCSports.com, Men's Health, USA Today, Cigar Magazine, CBS News Marketwatch, Newsweek,* and many others. A proud father of three young Little Leaguers, O'Connell lives with his family in Doylestown, Pennsylvania.